The Complete UK Air Fryer Cookbook for Beginners

Flavourful & Healthy Air Fryer Recipes for Every Meal | including Delicious Breakfast, Snacks, Dinner, Desserts & More

Sally J. Wilborn

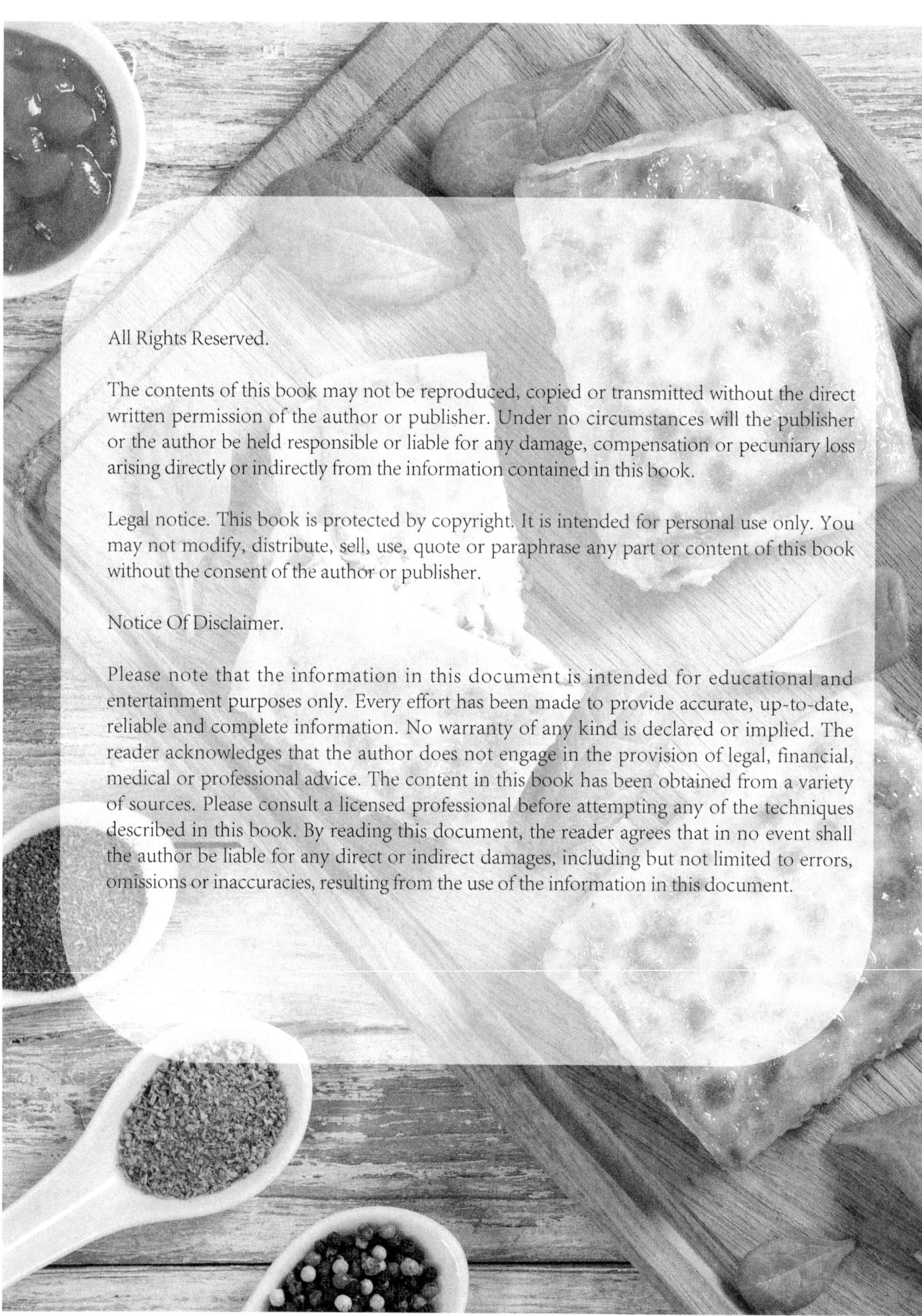

All Rights Reserved.

The contents of this book may not be reproduced, copied or transmitted without the direct written permission of the author or publisher. Under no circumstances will the publisher or the author be held responsible or liable for any damage, compensation or pecuniary loss arising directly or indirectly from the information contained in this book.

Legal notice. This book is protected by copyright. It is intended for personal use only. You may not modify, distribute, sell, use, quote or paraphrase any part or content of this book without the consent of the author or publisher.

Notice Of Disclaimer.

Please note that the information in this document is intended for educational and entertainment purposes only. Every effort has been made to provide accurate, up-to-date, reliable and complete information. No warranty of any kind is declared or implied. The reader acknowledges that the author does not engage in the provision of legal, financial, medical or professional advice. The content in this book has been obtained from a variety of sources. Please consult a licensed professional before attempting any of the techniques described in this book. By reading this document, the reader agrees that in no event shall the author be liable for any direct or indirect damages, including but not limited to errors, omissions or inaccuracies, resulting from the use of the information in this document.

TABLE OF CONTENT

BREAD AND BREAKFAST

Apple French Toast Sandwich 10

Pancake Muffins 10

Ham & Cheese Sandwiches 10

Granola 11

Holiday Breakfast Casserole 11

Egg & Bacon Pockets 12

Cheddar & Sausage Tater Tots 12

Hashbrown Potatoes Lyonnaise 13

Viking Toast 13

Crustless Broccoli, Roasted Pepper And Fontina Quiche 13

Meaty Omelet 14

Baked Eggs With Bacon-tomato Sauce. 14

Morning Burrito 15

Bacon Puff Pastry Pinwheels 15

Cinnamon Pear Oat Muffins 15

Huevos Rancheros 16

Morning Potato Cakes 16

Chorizo Biscuits 17

Tuscan Toast 17

Sweet-hot Pepperoni Pizza 17

Crispy Chicken Cakes 18

APPETIZERS AND SNACKS

Breaded Mozzarella Sticks 18

Smoked Whitefish Spread 19

Fried Olives 19

Baba Ghanouj 20

Spinach Cups 20

Greek Street Tacos 21

Cinnamon Apple Crisps 21

Sweet-and-salty Pretzels 21

Cheesy Zucchini Chips 22

Mozzarella Sticks 22

Spanish Fried Baby Squid 23

Basil Feta Crostini 23

Vegetarian Fritters With Green Dip .. 23

Barbecue Chicken Nachos 24

Crispy Chicken Bites With Gorgonzola Sauce 24

Crab Toasts 25

Sweet Potato Chips 25

Rich Clam Spread 26

Wrapped Shrimp Bites 26

Chicken Nachos 26

Fiery Sweet Chicken Wings 27

POULTRY RECIPES

Za'atar Chicken Drumsticks 27

Crispy Duck With Cherry Sauce 28

Fiesta Chicken Plate 28

Chicken Cordon Bleu Patties 29

Moroccan-style Chicken Strips 29

Spicy Black Bean Turkey Burgers With Cumin-avocado Spread 29

Pickle Brined Fried Chicken 30

Chicken Flautas 31

Chicken Salad With White Dressing . 31

Mom's Chicken Wings 32

Chicken Fried Steak With Gravy 32

Nashville Hot Chicken 33

Guajillo Chile Chicken Meatballs 33

Chicken Schnitzel Dogs 34

Sweet Chili Spiced Chicken 34

Asian-style Orange Chicken 35

Fiery Chicken Meatballs 35

Teriyaki Chicken Legs 36

Lemon Herb Whole Cornish Hen 36

Poblano Bake 36

Bacon & Chicken Flatbread 37

BEEF, PORK & LAMB RECIPES

Greek Pork Chops 37
Korean-style Lamb Shoulder Chops..38
Sirloin Steak Bites With Gravy 38
Perfect Pork Chops 39
Sloppy Joes 39
Balsamic Short Ribs 40
Pork Schnitzel 40
Honey Mesquite Pork Chops 41
Santorini Steak Bowls 41
Pork Chops 41
Venison Backstrap 42

Tuscan Veal Chops 42
Cal-mex Chimichangas 43
Pork Schnitzel With Dill Sauce 43
Flank Steak With Roasted Peppers And Chimichurri 44
Asy Carnitas 44
Chicken-fried Steak.........................45
German-style Pork Patties...............45
Meat Loaves 46
Pork Chops With Cereal Crust 46
Blossom Bbq Pork Chops 47

FISH AND SEAFOOD RECIPES

Shrimp Sliders With Avocado 47
Herb-crusted Sole...........................48
Tuna Nuggets In Hoisin Sauce 48
Fried Scallops 48

Crabmeat-stuffed Flounder 49
Crispy Fish Sandwiches...................49
Mediterranean Sea Scallops............50
Malaysian Shrimp With Sambal Mayo50

Oyster Shrimp With Fried Rice 51

Shrimp, Chorizo And Fingerling Potatoes 51

Summer Sea Scallops......................52

The Best Oysters Rockefeller 52

Crab Cakes On A Budget..................52

Cheese & Crab Stuffed Mushrooms .53

Kid's Flounder Fingers 53

Black Cod With Grapes, Fennel, Pecans And Kale 54

Panko-breaded Cod Fillets...............54

Sweet Potato–wrapped Shrimp........54

Corn & Shrimp Boil..........................55

Asian-style Salmon Fillets.................55

Breaded Parmesan Perch 56

VEGETARIAN RECIPES

Mexican Twice Air-fried Sweet Potatoes 56

Garlicky Roasted Mushrooms...........57

Charred Cauliflower Tacos................57

Caprese-style Sandwiches 58

Thai Peanut Veggie Burgers.............58

Balsamic Caprese Hasselback...........59

Spiced Vegetable Galette 59

Spinach & Brie Frittata 59

Rigatoni With Roasted Onions, Fennel, Spinach And Lemon Pepper Ricotta .60

Lentil Fritters 60

Sweet Roasted Carrots 61

Roasted Vegetable Thai Green Curry 61

Pesto Pepperoni Pizza Bread 62

Powerful Jackfruit Fritters 62

Roasted Vegetable, Brown Rice And Black Bean Burrito...........................62

Tex-mex Potatoes With Avocado Dressing..63

Fried Rice With Curried Tofu 63

Pinto Bean Casserole 64

Cheddar Stuffed Portobellos With Salsa 64

Thyme Meatless Patties 64

Vietnamese Gingered Tofu 65

VEGETABLE SIDE DISHES RECIPES

Simple Zucchini Ribbons.................... 66

Rich Spinach Chips............................ 66

Glazed Carrots 66

Brown Rice And Goat Cheese Croquettes.................................... 67

Garlicky Bell Pepper Mix................... 67

Spiced Pumpkin Wedges 68

Citrusy Brussels Sprouts 68

Roasted Yellow Squash And Onions . 68

Corn On The Cob 69

Hasselbacks 69

Smashed Fried Baby Potatoes 70

Shoestring Butternut Squash Fries ... 70

Mediterranean Roasted Vegetables . 70

Roasted Ratatouille Vegetables 71

Honey-roasted Parsnips.................... 71

Buttered Garlic Broccolini 72

Veggie Fritters 72

Roasted Brussels Sprouts 72

Lemony Green Bean Sauté 73

Honey-mustard Asparagus Puffs 73

Zucchini Fries................................... 73

SANDWICHES AND BURGERS RECIPES

Chicken Apple Brie Melt.................... 74

Reuben Sandwiches 75

Black Bean Veggie Burgers 75

Asian Glazed Meatballs 76

Chicken Saltimbocca Sandwiches..... 76

White Bean Veggie Burgers.............. 77

Mexican Cheeseburgers 77

Perfect Burgers 78

Chili Cheese Dogs 79
Salmon Burgers 79
Best-ever Roast Beef Sandwiches.....80
Inside Out Cheeseburgers 80
Sausage And Pepper Heros 81
Chicken Club Sandwiches 81
Eggplant Parmesan Subs 82

Thanksgiving Turkey Sandwiches......82
Philly Cheesesteak Sandwiches 83
Inside-out Cheeseburgers 83
Dijon Thyme Burgers 84
Lamb Burgers....................................85
Thai-style Pork Sliders 85

DESSERTS AND SWEETS

Mixed Berry Pie 86
Cheese Blintzes.................................86
Chocolate Rum Brownies 87
Magic Giant Chocolate Cookies........87
Cherry Cheesecake Rolls 87
Coconut Rice Cake 88
Holiday Pear Crumble.......................88
Peanut Butter-banana Roll-ups 89
Cinnamon Pear Cheesecake 89
Brown Sugar Baked Apples...............89
Rustic Berry Layer Cake 90

Peach Cobbler 90
Brownies With White Chocolate 91
Grilled Pineapple Dessert.................91
Homemade Chips Ahoy 91
Blueberry Cheesecake Tartlets 92
Fried Cannoli Wontons 92
Cinnamon Tortilla Crisps...................93
Blueberry Crisp.................................93
Guilty Chocolate Cookies..................93
Wild Blueberry Sweet Empanadas ...94

INDEX..95

INTRODUCTION

Are you a fan of air fryer recipes?
Are you tired of spending hours in the kitchen preparing meals for your family?
Do you want to enjoy crispy, delicious food without the guilt of deep frying?
Are you looking for a variety of recipes that cater to different tastes and dietary preferences?

If you answered yes to any of these questions, "Quick & Easy Air Fryer Cookbook UK" is the perfect solution for you!

Crispy, Healthy, and Affordable Delights: Discover 180 easy, tasty, and budget-friendly recipes, perfect for beginners and health enthusiasts. Enjoy crispy and delicious foods with maximum savings.
Effortless Cooking with Expert Tips: Whether you're a beginner or a cooking enthusiast, our tips and tricks make air frying a breeze. Follow our step-by-step guides to quickly prepare delicious meals, saving time and energy in the kitchen. Making tasty dishes has never been so simple.
Unleash Your Creativity with Versatile Recipes: Stimulate your creativity and experiment with our collection of recipes. From vegetables to irresistible desserts, each recipe is an open door to exploring new flavors, easily adaptable to meet different tastes and needs.

In addition, this book provides almost all food you can think of, such as:
 Breakfast dishes to start your day with zest
 Lunch options that are both satisfying and healthy
 Appetizers and snacks that are perfect for sharing
 Delicious dinners that make every night special
 Varieties of poultry recipes
 Seafood dishes that bring the ocean's freshness to your plate
 Perfect side dishes to round off your meals
 Decadent desserts for those sweet cravings
 And lots more…

Are you ready to say goodbye to excess oil and guilt-laden meals, welcoming simple, economical, and above all, delicious cooking?

Click BUY NOW and start your journey towards revolutionary cooking with air frying today!

Bread And Breakfast

Apple French Toast Sandwich

Servings: 1 | Prep Time: 10 Minutes | Cooking Time: 30 Minutes

Ingredients:

- 2 white bread slices
- 2 eggs
- 1 tsp cinnamon
- ½ peeled apple, sliced
- 1 tbsp brown sugar
- ¼ cup whipped cream

Directions:

1. Preheat air fryer to 177°C/350°F. Coat the apple slices with brown sugar in a small bowl. Whisk the eggs and cinnamon into a separate bowl until fluffy and completely blended. Coat the bread slices with the egg mixture, then place them on the greased frying basket. Top with apple slices and Air Fry for 20 minutes, flipping once until the bread is browned nicely and the apple is crispy.
2. Place one French toast slice onto a serving plate, then spoon the whipped cream on top and spread evenly. Scoop the caramelized apple slices onto the whipped cream, and cover with the second toast slice. Serve.

Variations & Ingredients Tips:

- Use brioche or challah bread for extra richness
- Add crushed nuts or granola to the sandwich
- Drizzle with maple syrup before serving

Per Serving: Calories: 455; Total Fat: 19g; Saturated Fat: 10g; Cholesterol: 290mg; Sodium: 370mg; Total Carbs: 62g; Dietary Fiber: 4g; Total Sugars: 28g; Protein: 13g

Pancake Muffins

Servings: 4 | Prep Time: 20 Minutes | Cooking Time: 8 Minutes

Ingredients:

- 1 cup flour
- 2 tbsp sugar (optional)
- 1/2 tsp baking soda
- 1 tsp baking powder
- 1/4 tsp salt
- 1 egg, beaten
- 1 cup buttermilk
- 2 tbsp melted butter
- 1 tsp vanilla extract
- 24 foil muffin cups
- Cooking spray
- Filling Suggestions:
- 1 tsp jelly/fruit preserves
- 1 tbsp or less fresh/frozen berries
- Dark chocolate chips
- Chopped nuts
- Cooked crumbled bacon/sausage

Directions:

1. In a bowl, mix flour, sugar, baking soda, powder and salt.
2. In another bowl, whisk egg, buttermilk, butter and vanilla.
3. Pour wet into dry ingredients and mix gently.
4. Grease foil cups and place 6 sets in air fryer basket.
5. Pour some batter into cups. Top with fillings, then more batter to 3/4 full.
6. Cook at 165°C/330°F for 8 mins.
7. Repeat to make remaining muffins.

Variations & Ingredients Tips:

- Use different milk like almond or oat milk.
- Add shredded cheese or herbs to the batter.
- Drizzle with maple syrup before serving.

Per Serving: Calories: 170; Total Fat: 6g; Saturated Fat: 3g; Cholesterol: 40mg; Sodium: 270mg; Total Carbs: 24g; Dietary Fiber: 1g; Sugars: 5g; Protein: 4g

Ham & Cheese Sandwiches

Servings: 2 | Prep Time: 5 Minutes | Cooking Time: 15 Minutes

Ingredients:

- 5 g butter
- 4 bread slices
- 4 deli ham slices
- 4 Cheddar cheese slices
- 4 thick tomato slices
- 1 teaspoon dried oregano

Directions:

1. Preheat air fryer to 190°C/370°F. Smear 2 g of butter on only one side of each slice of bread and sprinkle with oregano. On one of the slices, layer 2 slices of ham, 2 slices of cheese, and 2 slices of tomato on the unbuttered side. Place the unbuttered side of another piece of bread onto the toppings. Place the sandwiches butter side down into the air fryer. Bake for 8 minutes, flipping once until crispy. Let cool slightly, cut in half and serve.

Variations & Ingredients Tips:

- Use turkey, roast beef or salami instead of ham.
- Swap cheddar for Swiss, provolone or pepper Jack cheese.
- Add some sliced avocado, pickles or roasted red peppers for extra flavor.

Per Serving: Calories: 477; Total Fat: 28g; Saturated Fat: 15g; Cholesterol: 97mg; Sodium: 1477mg; Total Carbs: 29g; Dietary Fiber: 2g; Total Sugars: 6g; Protein: 29g

Granola

Servings: 2 | Preparation Time: 5 Minutes | Cooking Time: 40 Minutes

Ingredients:

- 1 cup rolled oats
- 3 tablespoons pure maple syrup
- 1 tablespoon sugar
- 1 tablespoon neutral-flavored oil, such as refined coconut, sunflower, or safflower
- 1/4 teaspoon sea salt
- 1/4 teaspoon ground cinnamon
- 1/4 teaspoon vanilla extract

Directions:

1. Insert the crisper plate into the basket and the basket into the unit. Preheat the unit by selecting BAKE, setting the temperature to 120°C/250°F, and set-ting the time to 3 minutes. Select START/STOP to begin.
2. In a medium bowl, stir together the oats, maple syrup, sugar, oil, salt, cinnamon, and vanilla until thoroughly combined. Transfer the granola to a 6-by-5-cm round baking pan.
3. Once the unit is preheated, place the pan into the basket.
4. Select BAKE, set the temperature to 120°C/250°F and set the time to 40 minutes. Select START/STOP to begin.
5. After 10 minutes, stir the granola well. Resume cooking, stirring the granola every 10 minutes, for a total of 40 minutes, or until the granola is lightly browned and mostly dry.
6. When the cooking is complete, place the granola on a plate to cool. It will become crisp as it cools. Store the completely cooled granola in an airtight container in a cool, dry place for 1 to 2 weeks.

Variations & Ingredients Tips:

- Use old-fashioned rolled oats for best texture.
- For clustered granola, avoid overstirring during baking.
- Let granola cool completely before storing for maximum crunchiness.

Per Serving: Calories: 330; Cholesterol: 0mg; Total Fat: 11g; Saturated Fat: 1.5g; Sodium: 155mg; Total Carbohydrates: 53g; Dietary Fiber: 4g; Total Sugars: 20g; Protein: 5g

Holiday Breakfast Casserole

Servings: 2 | Prep Time: 10 Minutes | Cooking Time: 25 Minutes

Ingredients:

- 59 g cooked spicy breakfast sausage
- 5 eggs
- 2 tablespoons heavy cream
- ½ teaspoon ground cumin
- Salt and pepper to taste
- 113 g feta cheese crumbles
- 1 tomato, diced
- 1 can green chiles, including juice
- 1 zucchini, diced

Directions:

1. Preheat air fryer to 165°C/325°F. Mix all ingredients in a bowl and pour into a greased baking pan. Place the

pan in the frying basket and Bake for 14 minutes. Let cool for 5 minutes before slicing. Serve right away.

Variations & Ingredients Tips:

- Use bacon, ham or chorizo instead of sausage.
- Add some sautéed onions, bell peppers or mushrooms to the mix.
- Top with sliced avocado, salsa or hot sauce before serving.

Per Serving: Calories: 498; Total Fat: 36g; Saturated Fat: 19g; Cholesterol: 543mg; Sodium: 1283mg; Total Carbs: 13g; Dietary Fiber: 3g; Total Sugars: 7g; Protein: 35g

Egg & Bacon Pockets

Servings: 4 | Prep Time: 30 Minutes | Cooking Time: 50 Minutes

Ingredients:

- 2 tablespoons olive oil
- 4 bacon slices, chopped
- ¼ red bell pepper, diced
- 1/3 cup scallions, chopped
- 4 eggs, beaten
- 1/3 cup grated Swiss cheese
- 1 cup flour
- 1½ teaspoons baking powder
- ½ teaspoon salt
- 1 cup Greek yogurt
- 1 egg white, beaten
- 2 teaspoons Italian seasoning
- 1 tablespoon Tabasco sauce

Directions:

1. Warm the olive oil in a skillet over medium heat and add the bacon. Stir-fry for 3-4 minutes or until crispy. Add the bell pepper and scallions and sauté for 3-4 minutes. Pour in the beaten eggs and stir-fry to scramble them, 3 minutes. Stir in the Swiss cheese and set aside to cool.
2. Sift the flour, baking powder, and salt in a bowl. Add yogurt and mix together until combined. Transfer the dough to a floured workspace. Knead it for 3 minutes or until smooth. Form the dough into 4 equal balls. Roll out the balls into round discs. Divide the bacon-egg mixture between the rounds. Fold the dough over the filling and seal the edges with a fork. Brush the pockets with egg white and sprinkle with Italian seasoning.
3. Preheat air fryer to 175°C/350°F. Arrange the pockets on the greased frying basket and Bake for 9-11 minutes, flipping once until golden. Serve with Tabasco sauce.

Variations & Ingredients Tips:

- Use sausage, ham or smoked salmon instead of bacon.
- Add sautéed mushrooms, spinach or sun-dried tomatoes to the egg mixture.
- Serve with salsa, hot sauce or ketchup for dipping.

Per Serving: Calories: 468; Total Fat: 26g; Saturated Fat: 8g; Cholesterol: 225mg; Sodium: 826mg; Total Carbs: 36g; Dietary Fiber: 1g; Total Sugars: 4g; Protein: 23g

Cheddar & Sausage Tater Tots

Servings: 4 | Prep Time: 10 Minutes | Cooking Time: 25 Minutes

Ingredients:

- 340g ground chicken sausage
- 4 eggs
- 1 cup sour cream
- 1 tsp Worcestershire sauce
- 1 tsp shallot powder
- Salt and pepper to taste
- 454g frozen tater tots
- ¾ cup grated cheddar

Directions:

1. Whisk eggs, sour cream, Worcestershire, shallot powder, salt and pepper in a bowl.
2. Brown sausage in a skillet 3-4 mins, breaking into pieces. Set aside.
3. Preheat air fryer to 165°C/330°F.
4. Lightly grease a baking pan. Layer tater tots in pan and air fry 6 mins, shaking pan.
5. Top tots with sausage and egg mixture. Air fry 6 more mins.
6. Sprinkle with cheddar and cook 2-3 more mins until melted.
7. Serve warm.

Variations & Ingredients Tips:

- Use pork or turkey sausage instead of chicken.
- Add diced peppers, onions or jalapeños to the mix.
- Substitute Greek yogurt for the sour cream.

Per Serving: Calories: 575; Total Fat: 35g; Saturated Fat:

13g; Cholesterol: 245mg; Sodium: 960mg; Total Carbs: 42g; Dietary Fiber: 3g; Total Sugars: 2g; Protein: 24g

Hashbrown Potatoes Lyonnaise

Servings: 4 | Prep Time: 10 Minutes | Cooking Time: 33 Minutes

Ingredients:

- 1 Vidalia (or other sweet) onion, sliced
- 1 teaspoon butter, melted
- 1 teaspoon brown sugar
- 2 large russet potatoes (about 454 g), sliced 1.3 cm thick
- 1 tablespoon vegetable oil
- salt and freshly ground black pepper

Directions:

1. Preheat the air fryer to 190°C/370°F.
2. Toss the sliced onions, melted butter and brown sugar together in the air fryer basket. Air-fry for 8 minutes, shaking the basket occasionally to help the onions cook evenly.
3. While the onions are cooking, bring a 3-quart saucepan of salted water to a boil on the stovetop. Par-cook the potatoes in boiling water for 3 minutes. Drain the potatoes and pat them dry with a clean kitchen towel.
4. Add the potatoes to the onions in the air fryer basket and drizzle with vegetable oil. Toss to coat the potatoes with the oil and season with salt and freshly ground black pepper.
5. Increase the air fryer temperature to 200°C/400°F and air-fry for 22 minutes tossing the vegetables a few times during the cooking time to help the potatoes brown evenly. Season to taste again with salt and freshly ground black pepper and serve warm.

Variations & Ingredients Tips:

- Add some chopped bacon, ham or pancetta to the onions for a meaty flavor.
- Sprinkle with chopped fresh herbs like parsley, chives or thyme before serving.
- Top with a dollop of sour cream or crème fraîche for a creamy finish.

Per Serving: Calories: 208; Total Fat: 6g; Saturated Fat: 2g; Cholesterol: 5mg; Sodium: 64mg; Total Carbs: 35g; Dietary Fiber: 3g; Total Sugars: 4g; Protein: 4g

Viking Toast

Servings: 2 | Prep Time: 10 Minutes | Cooking Time: 20 Minutes

Ingredients:

- 2 tbsp minced green chili pepper
- 1 avocado, pressed
- 1 clove garlic, minced
- ¼ tsp lemon juice
- Salt and pepper to taste
- 2 bread slices
- 2 plum tomatoes, sliced
- 115g smoked salmon
- ¼ diced peeled red onion

Directions:

1. Preheat air fryer at 175°C/350°F.
2. Combine the avocado, garlic, lemon juice, and salt in a bowl until you reach your desired consistency.
3. Spread avocado mixture on the bread slices.
4. Top with tomato slices and sprinkle with black pepper.
5. Place bread slices in the frying basket and Bake for 5 minutes.
6. Transfer to a plate. Top each bread slice with salmon, green chili pepper, and red onion.
7. Serve.

Variations & Ingredients Tips:

- Use whole grain or sourdough bread for extra fiber.
- Substitute smoked trout or gravlax for the salmon.
- Add sliced hard-boiled eggs or sprouts on top.

Per Serving: Calories: 335; Total Fat: 17g; Saturated Fat: 3g; Cholesterol: 30mg; Sodium: 660mg; Total Carbs: 26g; Dietary Fiber: 8g; Total Sugars: 5g; Protein: 19g

Crustless Broccoli, Roasted Pepper And Fontina Quiche

Servings: 4 | Prep Time: 10 Minutes | Cooking Time: 60 Minutes

Ingredients:

- 18 cm cake pan
- 1 cup broccoli florets
- ¾ cup chopped roasted red peppers
- 150 g grated Fontina cheese
- 6 eggs

- ¾ cup heavy cream
- ½ teaspoon salt
- Freshly ground black pepper

Directions:

1. Preheat the air fryer to 180°C/360°F.
2. Grease the inside of an 18 cm cake pan (10 cm deep) or other oven-safe pan that will fit into your air fryer. Place the broccoli florets and roasted red peppers in the cake pan and top with the grated Fontina cheese.
3. Whisk the eggs and heavy cream together in a bowl. Season the eggs with salt and freshly ground black pepper. Pour the egg mixture over the cheese and vegetables and cover the pan with aluminum foil. Transfer the cake pan to the air fryer basket.
4. Air-fry at 180°C/360°F for 60 minutes. Remove the aluminum foil for the last two minutes of cooking time.
5. Unmold the quiche onto a platter and cut it into slices to serve with a side salad or perhaps some air-fried potatoes.

Variations & Ingredients Tips:

- Use different types of vegetables, such as spinach or mushrooms, for a variety of flavors and textures.
- Add some cooked bacon or ham to the quiche for a meaty twist.
- For a lighter version, replace the heavy cream with milk or half-and-half.

Per Serving: Calories: 400; Total Fat: 32g; Saturated Fat: 18g; Cholesterol: 345mg; Sodium: 610mg; Total Carbs: 6g; Fiber: 1g; Sugars: 3g; Protein: 22g

Meaty Omelet

Servings: 4 | Prep Time: 5 Minutes | Cooking Time: 20 Minutes

Ingredients:

- 6 eggs
- 1/2 cup grated Swiss cheese
- 3 breakfast sausages, sliced
- 8 bacon strips, sliced
- Salt and pepper to taste

Directions:

1. Preheat air fryer to 180°C/360°F.
2. In a bowl, beat the eggs and stir in Swiss cheese, sausages and bacon.
3. Transfer the mixture to a baking dish and set in the fryer.
4. Bake for 15 minutes or until golden and crisp.
5. Season and serve.

Variations & Ingredients Tips:

- Add some diced bell peppers, onions or mushrooms to the mix.
- Use cheddar, feta or goat cheese instead of Swiss.
- Serve with salsa, hot sauce or ketchup on the side.

Per Serving: Calories: 370; Total Fat: 29g; Saturated Fat: 12g; Cholesterol: 405mg; Sodium: 670mg; Total Carbs: 1g; Dietary Fiber: 0g; Total Sugars: 1g; Protein: 26g

Baked Eggs With Bacon-tomato Sauce

Servings: 1 | Prep Time: 10 Minutes | Cooking Time: 12 Minutes

Ingredients:

- 1 teaspoon olive oil
- 2 tablespoons finely chopped onion
- 1 teaspoon chopped fresh oregano
- Pinch crushed red pepper flakes
- 1 (400g) can crushed or diced tomatoes
- Salt and freshly ground black pepper
- 2 slices bacon, chopped
- 2 large eggs
- ¼ cup grated Cheddar cheese
- Fresh parsley, chopped

Directions:

1. Make tomato sauce: Sauté onion, oregano and pepper flakes in oil for 5 mins. Add tomatoes, salt, pepper and simmer 10 mins.
2. Preheat air fryer to 205°C/400°F. Add a little water to drawer bottom.
3. Air fry bacon 5 mins until crispy. Drain grease from drawer.
4. Transfer sauce to a 18cm pie dish. Crack eggs over sauce and scatter bacon on top. Season with salt and pepper.
5. Air fry at 205°C/400°F for 5 mins until eggs are nearly set. Top with cheese and cook 2 more mins to melt.
6. Garnish with parsley and let cool slightly before serving.

Variations & Ingredients Tips:

- Use turkey or plant-based bacon.
- Add sautéed vegetables to the sauce.
- Substitute feta or goat cheese for the cheddar.

Per Serving: Calories: 335; Total Fat: 21g; Saturated Fat: 8g; Cholesterol: 330mg; Sodium: 630mg; Total Carbs: 18g; Dietary Fiber: 3g; Total Sugars: 8g; Protein: 20g

Morning Burrito

Servings: 4 | Prep Time: 10 Minutes | Cooking Time: 15 Minutes

Ingredients:

- 56-g cheddar cheese, torn into pieces
- 2 hard-boiled eggs, chopped
- 1 avocado, chopped
- 1 red bell pepper, chopped
- 3 tbsp salsa
- 4 flour tortillas

Directions:

1. Whisk the eggs, avocado, red bell pepper, salsa, and cheese.
2. Pour the tortillas on a clean surface and divide the egg mix between them.
3. Fold the edges and roll up; poke a toothpick through so they hold.
4. Preheat air fryer to 200°C/390°F.
5. Place the burritos in the frying basket and Air Fry for 3-5 minutes until crispy and golden.
6. Serve hot.

Variations & Ingredients Tips:

- Add cooked potatoes, bacon or chorizo to the filling.
- Use whole wheat or spinach tortillas for extra nutrition.
- Serve with sour cream, guacamole or extra salsa on the side.

Per Serving: Calories: 320; Total Fat: 18g; Saturated Fat: 6g; Cholesterol: 155mg; Sodium: 480mg; Total Carbs: 28g; Dietary Fiber: 5g; Sugars: 3g; Protein: 12g

Bacon Puff Pastry Pinwheels

Servings: 8 | Prep Time: 15 Minutes | Cooking Time: 10 Minutes

Ingredients:

- 1 sheet puff pastry
- 2 tablespoons maple syrup
- ¼ cup brown sugar
- 8 slices bacon (not thick cut)
- Coarsely cracked black pepper
- Vegetable oil

Directions:

1. On a lightly floured surface, roll puff pastry into a 25x28cm square. Cut into 8 strips.
2. Brush pastry with maple syrup and sprinkle with brown sugar, leaving 5cm exposed at ends.
3. Place a bacon slice on each strip, letting 0.3cm hang over. Season generously with pepper.
4. Roll pastry and bacon into pinwheels. Seal ends with water.
5. Preheat air fryer to 182°C/360°F.
6. Brush basket with oil. Add pinwheels and air fry 8 minutes. Flip and cook 2 more minutes.
7. Serve warm.

Variations & Ingredients Tips:

- Use turkey or beef bacon instead.
- Sprinkle with grated parmesan before rolling.
- Dip in maple or ranch dressing for serving.

Per Serving: Calories: 230; Total Fat: 12g; Saturated Fat: 4g; Cholesterol: 15mg; Sodium: 410mg; Total Carbs: 24g; Dietary Fiber: 1g; Total Sugars: 8g; Protein: 6g

Cinnamon Pear Oat Muffins

Servings: 6 | Prep Time: 10 Minutes | Cooking Time: 30 Minutes + Cooling Time

Ingredients:

- ½ cup apple sauce
- 1 large egg
- ⅓ cup brown sugar
- 2 tablespoons butter, melted
- ½ cup milk
- 133 g rolled oats
- 1 teaspoon ground cinnamon
- ½ teaspoon baking powder
- Pinch of salt
- ½ cup diced peeled pears

Directions:

1. Preheat the air fryer to 180°C/350°F.
2. Place the apple sauce, egg, brown sugar, melted butter,

and milk into a bowl and mix to combine.
3. Stir in the oats, cinnamon, baking powder, and salt and mix well, then fold in the pears.
4. Grease 6 silicone muffin cups with baking spray, then spoon the batter in equal portions into the cups.
5. Put the muffin cups in the frying basket and Bake for 13-18 minutes or until set.
6. Leave to cool for 15 minutes. Serve.

Variations & Ingredients Tips:

- Use different types of fruit, such as apples or bananas, for a variety of flavors.
- Add some chopped nuts, such as pecans or walnuts, for a crunchy texture.
- For a sweeter version, add some honey or maple syrup to the batter.

Per Serving: Calories: 220; Total Fat: 7g; Saturated Fat: 3.5g; Cholesterol: 40mg; Sodium: 120mg; Total Carbs: 36g; Fiber: 4g; Sugars: 16g; Protein: 5g

Huevos Rancheros

Servings: 4 | Prep Time: 10 Minutes | Cooking Time: 45 Minutes + Cooling Time

Ingredients:

- 1 tablespoon olive oil
- 20 cherry tomatoes, halved
- 2 chopped plum tomatoes
- 59 ml tomato sauce
- 2 scallions, sliced
- 2 garlic cloves, minced
- 1 teaspoon honey
- ½ teaspoon salt
- ⅛ teaspoon cayenne pepper
- ¼ teaspoon grated nutmeg
- ¼ teaspoon paprika
- 4 eggs

Directions:

1. Preheat the air fryer to 190°C/370°F. Combine the olive oil, cherry tomatoes, plum tomatoes, tomato sauce, scallions, garlic, nutmeg, honey, salt, paprika and cayenne in an 18 cm springform pan that has been wrapped in foil to prevent leaks. Put the pan in the frying basket and Bake the mix for 15-20 minutes, stirring twice until the tomatoes are soft. Mash some of the tomatoes in the pan with a fork, then stir them into the sauce. Also, break the eggs into the sauce, then return the pan to the fryer and Bake for 2 minutes. Remove the pan from the fryer and stir the eggs into the sauce, whisking them through the sauce. Don't mix in completely. Cook for 4-8 minutes more or until the eggs are set. Let cool, then serve.

Variations & Ingredients Tips:

- Serve with warm corn tortillas, refried beans and sliced avocado.
- Top with crumbled queso fresco or cotija cheese.
- Add some chopped jalapeños or chipotle peppers for extra heat.

Per Serving: Calories: 164; Total Fat: 11g; Saturated Fat: 3g; Cholesterol: 186mg; Sodium: 425mg; Total Carbs: 10g; Dietary Fiber: 2g; Total Sugars: 6g; Protein: 8g

Morning Potato Cakes

Servings: 6 | Prep Time: 15 Minutes | Cooking Time: 50 Minutes

Ingredients:

- 4 Yukon Gold potatoes
- 2 cups kale, chopped
- 1 cup rice flour
- 1/4 cup cornstarch
- 3/4 cup milk
- 2 tbsp lemon juice
- 2 tsp dried rosemary
- 2 tsp shallot powder
- Salt and pepper to taste
- 1/2 tsp turmeric powder

Directions:

1. Preheat air fryer to 200°C/390°F.
2. Scrub and bake whole potatoes for 30 mins until soft.
3. Chop and mash potatoes. Mix with kale, flours, milk, lemon, spices, salt & pepper.
4. Form into 12 patties.
5. Grease air fryer basket and cook patties in batches for 10-12 mins, flipping once, until golden brown.
6. Serve warm.

Variations & Ingredients Tips:

- Add shredded cheese, bacon bits or chopped onions.
- Substitute cauliflower, zucchini or carrots for some of the potatoes.
- Use gluten-free flour if needed.

Per Serving: Calories: 140; Total Fat: 1g; Saturated Fat: 0g; Cholesterol: 1mg; Sodium: 70mg; Total Carbs: 30g; Dietary Fiber: 3g; Sugars: 2g; Protein: 3g

Chorizo Biscuits

Servings: 4 | Prep Time: 5 Minutes | Cooking Time: 20 Minutes

Ingredients:

- 340 g chorizo sausage
- 1 can biscuits
- ⅛ cup cream cheese

Directions:

1. Preheat air fryer to 190°C/370°F.
2. Shape the sausage into 4 patties. Bake in the air fryer for 10 minutes, turning once halfway through. Remove and set aside.
3. Separate the biscuit dough into 5 biscuits, then place in the air fryer for 5 minutes, flipping once. Remove from the air fryer. Divide each biscuit in half.
4. Smear 1 teaspoon of cream cheese on the bottom half, top with the sausage, and then cover with the top half. Serve warm.

Variations & Ingredients Tips:

▷ Use different types of sausage, such as Italian or breakfast sausage, for a variety of flavors.
▷ Add some sliced jalapeños or hot sauce to the cream cheese for a spicy kick.
▷ Serve the chorizo biscuits with a side of salsa or guacamole for a Mexican-inspired breakfast sandwich.

Per Serving: Calories: 580; Total Fat: 46g; Saturated Fat: 17g; Cholesterol: 95mg; Sodium: 1420mg; Total Carbs: 23g; Fiber: 1g; Sugars: 3g; Protein: 22g

Tuscan Toast

Servings: 4 | Prep Time: 5 Minutes | Cooking Time: 5 Minutes

Ingredients:

- ¼ cup butter
- ½ teaspoon lemon juice
- ½ clove garlic
- ½ teaspoon dried parsley flakes
- 4 slices Italian bread, 2.5cm thick

Directions:

1. Place butter, lemon juice, garlic, and parsley in a food processor. Process about 1 minute, or until garlic is pulverized and ingredients are well blended.
2. Spread garlic butter on both sides of bread slices.
3. Place bread slices upright in air fryer basket. (They can lie flat but cook better standing on end.)
4. Cook at 200°C/390°F for 5 minutes or until toasty brown.

Variations & Ingredients Tips:

▷ Add grated parmesan or crushed red pepper to the butter mixture.
▷ Use sourdough or ciabatta bread instead of Italian.
▷ Sprinkle with dried herbs like rosemary or oregano before serving.

Per Serving: Calories: 186; Total Fat: 12g; Saturated Fat: 7g; Cholesterol: 31mg; Sodium: 247mg; Total Carbs: 17g; Dietary Fiber: 1g; Total Sugars: 1g; Protein: 4g

Sweet-hot Pepperoni Pizza

Servings: 2 | Prep Time: 8 Minutes | Cooking Time: 18 Minutes

Ingredients:

- 1 (170-225g) pizza dough ball*
- Olive oil
- 1/2 cup pizza sauce
- 3/4 cup grated mozzarella cheese
- 1/2 cup thick sliced pepperoni
- 1/3 cup sliced pickled hot banana peppers
- 1/4 teaspoon dried oregano
- 2 teaspoons honey

Directions:

1. Preheat air fryer to 200°C/390°F.
2. Cut out a piece of aluminum foil the same size as the bottom of the air fryer basket. Brush the foil circle with olive oil. Shape the dough into a circle and place it on top of the foil. Dock the dough by piercing it several times with a fork. Brush the dough lightly with olive oil and transfer it into the air fryer basket with the foil on the bottom.
3. Air-fry the plain pizza dough for 6 minutes. Turn the dough over, remove the aluminum foil and brush again with olive oil. Air-fry for an additional 4 minutes.
4. Spread the pizza sauce on top of the dough and sprinkle the mozzarella cheese over the sauce. Top with the

pepperoni, pepper slices and dried oregano. Lower the temperature of the air fryer to 175°C/350°F and cook for 8 minutes, until the cheese has melted and lightly browned. Transfer the pizza to a cutting board and drizzle with the honey. Slice and serve.

Variations & Ingredients Tips:

- Use store-bought or homemade dough.
- Add other toppings like mushrooms, onions, olives.
- Sprinkle with parmesan or red pepper flakes before baking.

Per Serving: Calories: 570; Total Fat: 28g; Saturated Fat: 10g; Cholesterol: 55mg; Sodium: 1310mg; Total Carbs: 57g; Dietary Fiber: 3g; Total Sugars: 9g; Protein: 22g

Crispy Chicken Cakes

Servings: 4 | Prep Time: 10 Minutes | Cooking Time: 30 Minutes

Ingredients:

- 1 peeled Granny Smith apple, chopped
- 2 scallions, chopped
- 3 tablespoons ground almonds
- 1 teaspoon garlic powder
- 1 egg white
- 2 tablespoons apple juice
- Black pepper to taste
- 450 g ground chicken

Directions:

1. Preheat air fryer to 165°C/330°F.
2. Combine the apple, scallions, almonds, garlic powder, egg white, apple juice, and pepper in a bowl. Add the ground chicken using your hands. Mix well.
3. Make 8 patties and set four in the frying basket. Air Fry for 8-12 minutes until crispy. Repeat with the remaining patties.
4. Serve hot.

Variations & Ingredients Tips:

- Use different types of ground meat, such as turkey or pork, for a variety of flavors.
- Add some grated Parmesan cheese or bread crumbs to the patty mixture for extra flavor and texture.
- Serve the chicken cakes with a side of salsa or tzatziki sauce for dipping.

Per Serving: Calories: 240; Total Fat: 14g; Saturated Fat: 3.5g; Cholesterol: 115mg; Sodium: 120mg; Total Carbs: 6g; Fiber: 1g; Sugars: 4g; Protein: 26g

Appetizers And Snacks

Breaded Mozzarella Sticks

Servings: 6 | Prep Time: 15 Minutes | Cooking Time: 25 Minutes

Ingredients:

- 2 tbsp flour
- 1 egg
- 1 tbsp milk
- ½ cup bread crumbs
- ¼ tsp salt
- ¼ tsp Italian seasoning
- 10 mozzarella sticks
- 2 tsp olive oil
- ½ cup warm marinara sauce

Directions:

1. Place the flour in a bowl. In another bowl, beat the egg and milk. In a third bowl, combine the crumbs, salt, and Italian seasoning. Cut the mozzarella sticks into thirds. Roll each piece in flour, then dredge in egg mixture, and finally roll in breadcrumb mixture. Shake off the excess between each step. Place them in the freezer

for 10 minutes.
2. Preheat air fryer to 200°C/400°F. Place mozzarella sticks in the frying basket and Air Fry for 5 minutes, shake twice and brush with olive oil. Serve the mozzarella sticks immediately with marinara sauce.

Variations & Ingredients Tips:

- Use panko breadcrumbs for a crispier coating.
- Add some garlic powder or Parmesan cheese to the breadcrumb mixture.
- Serve with ranch dressing or pesto for dipping.

Per Serving: Calories: 160; Total Fat: 10g; Saturated Fat: 5g; Cholesterol: 49mg; Sodium: 471mg; Total Carbs: 10g; Dietary Fiber: 1g; Total Sugars: 2g; Protein: 9g

Smoked Whitefish Spread

Servings: 1 | Prep Time: 150 Minutes | Cooking Time: 10 Minutes

Ingredients:

- 340 g boneless skinless white-flesh fish fillets, such as hake or trout
- 3 tablespoons liquid smoke
- 3 tablespoons regular, low-fat, or fat-free mayonnaise (gluten-free, if a concern)
- 2 teaspoons jarred prepared white horseradish (optional)
- ¼ teaspoon onion powder
- ¼ teaspoon celery seeds
- ¼ teaspoon table salt
- ¼ teaspoon ground black pepper

Directions:

1. Put the fish fillets in a zip-closed bag, add the liquid smoke, and seal closed. Rub the liquid smoke all over the fish, then refrigerate the sealed bag for 2 hours.
2. Preheat the air fryer to 200°C/400°F.
3. Set a 30 cm piece of aluminum foil on your work surface. Remove the fish fillets from the bag and set them in the center of this piece of foil (the fillets can overlap). Fold the long sides of the foil together and crimp them closed. Make a tight seam so no steam can escape. Fold up the ends and crimp to seal well.
4. Set the packet in the basket and air-fry undisturbed for 10 minutes.
5. Use kitchen tongs to transfer the foil packet to a wire rack. Cool for a minute or so. Open the packet, transfer the fish to a plate, and refrigerate for 30 minutes.
6. Put the cold fish in a food processor. Add the mayonnaise, horseradish (if using), onion powder, celery seeds, salt, and pepper. Cover and pulse to a slightly coarse spread, certainly not fully smooth.
7. For a more traditional texture, put the fish fillets in a bowl, add the other ingredients, and stir with a wooden spoon, mashing the fish with everything else to make a coarse paste.
8. Scrape the spread into a bowl and serve at once, or cover with plastic wrap and store in the fridge for up to 4 days.

Variations & Ingredients Tips:

- Use smoked fish instead of fresh fish and liquid smoke for a more intense smoky flavor.
- Add some chopped fresh herbs, like parsley or chives, to the spread for extra flavor.
- Serve the spread with crackers, crostini, or raw vegetables for dipping.

Per Serving: Calories: 320; Total Fat: 20g; Saturated Fat: 3g; Cholesterol: 95mg; Sodium: 1180mg; Total Carbs: 2g; Fiber: 0g; Sugars: 0g; Protein: 32g

Fried Olives

Servings: 5 | Prep Time: 15 Minutes | Cooking Time: 10 Minutes

Ingredients:

- ⅓ cup All-purpose flour or tapioca flour
- 1 Large egg white(s)
- 1 tablespoon Brine from the olive jar
- ⅔ cup Plain dried bread crumbs (gluten-free, if a concern)
- 15 Large pimiento-stuffed green olives
- Olive oil spray

Directions:

1. Preheat the air fryer to 200°C/400°F.
2. Pour the flour in a medium-size zip-closed plastic bag. Whisk the egg white and pickle brine in a medium bowl until foamy. Spread out the bread crumbs on a dinner plate.
3. Pour all the olives into the bag with the flour, seal, and shake to coat the olives. Remove a couple of olives, shake off any excess flour, and drop them into the egg white mixture. Toss gently but well to coat. Pick them up one at a time and roll each in the bread crumbs until well coated on all sides, even the ends. Set them aside

on a cutting board as you finish the rest. When done, coat the olives with olive oil spray on all sides.
4. Place the olives in the basket in one layer. Air-fry for 8 minutes, gently shaking the basket once halfway through the cooking process to rearrange the olives, until lightly browned.
5. Gently pour the olives onto a wire rack and cool for at least 10 minutes before serving. Once cooled, the olives may be stored in a sealed container in the fridge for up to 2 days. To rewarm them, set them in the basket of a heated 200°C/400°F air fryer undisturbed for 2 minutes.

Variations & Ingredients Tips:

- Use blue cheese, feta or almond-stuffed olives for different fillings.
- Add some smoked paprika, garlic powder or dried herbs to the breading.
- Serve as a garnish for martinis or bloody marys.

Per Serving: Calories: 120; Total Fat: 8g; Saturated Fat: 1g; Cholesterol: 0mg; Sodium: 516mg; Total Carbs: 9g; Dietary Fiber: 1g; Total Sugars: 1g; Protein: 2g

Baba Ghanouj

Servings: 2 | Prep Time: 10 Minutes | Cooking Time: 40 Minutes

Ingredients:

- 2 Small (340 g) purple Italian eggplant(s)
- ¼ cup Olive oil
- ¼ cup Tahini
- ½ teaspoon Ground black pepper
- ¼ teaspoon Onion powder
- ¼ teaspoon Mild smoked paprika (optional)
- Up to 1 teaspoon Table salt

Directions:

1. Preheat the air fryer to 200°C/400°F.
2. Prick the eggplant(s) on all sides with a fork. When the machine is at temperature, set the eggplant(s) in the basket in one layer. Air-fry undisturbed for 40 minutes, or until blackened and soft.
3. Remove the basket from the machine. Cool the eggplant(s) in the basket for 20 minutes.
4. Use a nonstick-safe spatula, and perhaps a flatware tablespoon for balance, to gently transfer the eggplant(s) to a bowl. The juices will run out. Make sure the bowl is close to the basket. Split the eggplant(s) open.
5. Scrape the soft insides of half an eggplant into a food processor. Repeat with the remaining piece(s). Add any juices from the bowl to the eggplant in the food processor, but discard the skins and stems.
6. Add the olive oil, tahini, pepper, onion powder, and smoked paprika (if using). Add about half the salt, then cover and process until smooth, stopping the machine at least once to scrape down the inside of the canister. Check the spread for salt and add more as needed. Scrape the baba ghanouj into a bowl and serve warm, or set aside at room temperature for up to 2 hours, or cover and store in the refrigerator for up to 4 days.

Variations & Ingredients Tips:

- Add some minced garlic or roasted garlic for extra flavor.
- Top with a drizzle of olive oil and a sprinkle of smoked paprika before serving.
- Serve with pita chips, crudités or as a spread for sandwiches.

Per Serving: Calories: 397; Total Fat: 36g; Saturated Fat: 5g; Cholesterol: 0mg; Sodium: 1188mg; Total Carbs: 18g; Dietary Fiber: 9g; Total Sugars: 9g; Protein: 6g

Spinach Cups

Servings: 30 | Prep Time: 15 minutes | Cooking Time: 5 Minutes

Ingredients:

- 1 170-g can crabmeat, drained to yield 80 ml meat
- 60 g frozen spinach, thawed, drained, and chopped
- 1 clove garlic, minced
- ½ cup grated Parmesan cheese
- 3 tbsp plain yogurt
- ¼ tsp lemon juice
- ½ tsp Worcestershire sauce
- 30 mini phyllo shells (2 boxes of 15 each), thawed
- cooking spray

Directions:

1. Remove any bits of shell that might remain in the crabmeat. Mix crabmeat, spinach, garlic, and cheese together. Stir in the yogurt, lemon juice, and Worcestershire sauce and mix well. Spoon a teaspoon of filling into each phyllo shell. Spray air fryer basket and arrange

half the shells in the basket. Cook at 200°C/390°F for 5 minutes. Repeat with remaining shells.

Variations & Ingredients Tips:

- Substitute cooked, chopped shrimp or smoked salmon for the crabmeat.
- Add a pinch of cayenne pepper, Old Bay seasoning, or dill weed to the filling for extra flavor.
- Garnish with fresh parsley, chives, or a small dollop of sour cream before serving.

Per Serving: Calories: 39; Total Fat: 2g; Saturated Fat: 1g; Cholesterol: 7mg; Sodium: 74mg; Total Carbohydrates: 3g; Dietary Fiber: 0g; Total Sugars: 0g; Protein: 2g

Greek Street Tacos

Servings: 8 | Prep Time: 10 Minutes | Cooking Time: 3 Minutes

Ingredients:

- 8 small flour tortillas (10 cm diameter)
- 8 tablespoons hummus
- 4 tablespoons crumbled feta cheese
- 4 tablespoons chopped kalamata or other olives (optional)
- olive oil for misting

Directions:

1. Place 1 tablespoon of hummus or tapenade in the center of each tortilla. Top with 1 teaspoon of feta crumbles and 1 teaspoon of chopped olives, if using.
2. Using your finger or a small spoon, moisten the edges of the tortilla all around with water.
3. Fold tortilla over to make a half-moon shape. Press center gently. Then press the edges firmly to seal in the filling.
4. Mist both sides with olive oil.
5. Place in air fryer basket very close but try not to overlap.
6. Cook at 200°C/390°F for 3 minutes, just until lightly browned and crispy.

Variations & Ingredients Tips:

- Use pita bread, naan or flatbread instead of tortillas.
- Add some diced tomatoes, cucumbers or red onions to the filling.
- Drizzle with tzatziki sauce, balsamic glaze or hot sauce before serving.

Per Serving: Calories: 125; Total Fat: 5g; Saturated Fat: 1g; Cholesterol: 6mg; Sodium: 263mg; Total Carbs: 17g; Dietary Fiber: 1g; Total Sugars: 0g; Protein: 4g

Cinnamon Apple Crisps

Servings: 1 | Prep Time: 10 Minutes | Cooking Time: 22 Minutes

Ingredients:

- 1 large apple
- ½ teaspoon ground cinnamon
- 2 teaspoons avocado oil or coconut oil

Directions:

1. Preheat the air fryer to 150°C/300°F.
2. Using a mandolin or knife, slice the apples to 6 mm thickness. Pat the apples dry with a paper towel or kitchen cloth. Sprinkle the apple slices with ground cinnamon. Spray or drizzle the oil over the top of the apple slices and toss to coat.
3. Place the apple slices in the air fryer basket. To allow for even cooking, don't overlap the slices; cook in batches if necessary.
4. Cook for 20 minutes, shaking the basket every 5 minutes. After 20 minutes, increase the air fryer temperature to 165°C/330°F and cook another 2 minutes, shaking the basket every 30 seconds. Remove the apples from the basket before they get too dark.
5. Spread the chips out onto paper towels to cool completely, at least 5 minutes. Repeat with the remaining apple slices until they're all cooked.

Variations & Ingredients Tips:

- Use pears or peaches instead of apples.
- Sprinkle with pumpkin pie spice or apple pie spice for extra flavor.
- Serve with vanilla yogurt or ice cream for dipping.

Per Serving: Calories: 175; Total Fat: 14g; Saturated Fat: 2g; Cholesterol: 0mg; Sodium: 2mg; Total Carbs: 15g; Dietary Fiber: 4g; Total Sugars: 10g; Protein: 1g

Sweet-and-salty Pretzels

Servings: 4 | Prep Time: 5 Minutes | Cooking Time: 5 Minutes

Ingredients:

- 2 cups plain pretzel nuggets
- 1 tbsp Worcestershire sauce
- 2 tsp granulated white sugar
- 1 tsp mild smoked paprika
- ½ tsp garlic or onion powder

Directions:

1. Preheat the air fryer to 175°C/350°F. Put the pretzel nuggets, Worcestershire sauce, sugar, smoked paprika, and garlic or onion powder in a large bowl. Toss gently until the nuggets are well coated. When the machine is at temperature, pour the nuggets into the basket, spreading them into as close to a single layer as possible. Air-fry, shaking the basket three or four times to rearrange the nuggets, for 5 minutes, or until the nuggets are toasted and aromatic. Although the coating will darken, don't let it burn, especially if the machine's temperature is 180°C/360°F. Pour the nuggets onto a wire rack and gently spread them into one layer. (A rubber spatula does a good job.) Cool for 5 minutes before serving.

Variations & Ingredients Tips:

- Experiment with different spice blends like ranch seasoning, taco seasoning, or Italian herbs.
- Add a pinch of cayenne pepper or red pepper flakes for a spicy kick.
- Drizzle with melted chocolate or caramel for a sweet and salty treat.

Per Serving: Calories: 113; Total Fat: 1g; Saturated Fat: 0g; Sodium: 504mg; Total Carbohydrates: 24g; Dietary Fiber: 1g; Total Sugars: 3g; Protein: 3g

Cheesy Zucchini Chips

Servings: 4 | Prep Time: 20 Minutes | Cooking Time: 35 Minutes

Ingredients:

- 450 g thin zucchini chips
- 2 eggs
- ½ cup bread crumbs
- ½ cup grated Pecorino cheese
- Salt and pepper to taste
- ½ cup mayonnaise
- ½ tbsp olive oil
- ½ lemon. juiced
- 1 tsp garlic powder
- Salt and pepper to taste

Directions:

1. Preheat air fryer to 175°C/350°F. Beat eggs in a small bowl, then set aside. In another small bowl, stir together bread crumbs, Pecorino, salt, and pepper. Dip zucchini slices into the egg mixture, then in the crumb mixture. Place them in the greased frying basket and Air Fry for 10 minutes. Remove and set aside to cool. Mix the mayonnaise, olive oil, lemon juice, garlic, salt, and pepper in a bowl to make aioli. Serve aioli with chips and enjoy.

Variations & Ingredients Tips:

- Use yellow squash or eggplant slices instead of zucchini.
- Add some smoked paprika or Italian seasoning to the breadcrumb mixture.
- Serve with marinara sauce or ranch dressing for dipping.

Per Serving: Calories: 313; Total Fat: 24g; Saturated Fat: 6g; Cholesterol: 111mg; Sodium: 513mg; Total Carbs: 15g; Dietary Fiber: 2g; Total Sugars: 4g; Protein: 11g

Mozzarella Sticks

Servings: 4 | Prep Time: 10 Minutes | Cooking Time: 5 Minutes

Ingredients:

- 1 egg
- 1 tbsp water
- 8 eggroll wraps
- 8 mozzarella string cheese "sticks"
- sauce for dipping

Directions:

1. Beat together egg and water in a small bowl. Lay out egg roll wraps and moisten edges with egg wash. Place one piece of string cheese on each wrap near one end. Fold in sides of egg roll wrap over ends of cheese, and then roll up. Brush outside of wrap with egg wash and press gently to seal well. Place in air fryer basket in single layer and cook at 200°C/390°F for 5 minutes. Cook an additional 1 or 2 minutes, if necessary, until they are golden brown and crispy. Serve with your favorite dipping sauce.

Variations & Ingredients Tips:

- Use wonton wrappers instead of egg roll wraps for a

- lighter, crispier texture.
- ▶ Experiment with different types of cheese like cheddar, pepper jack, or gouda.
- ▶ Serve with ranch dressing, marinara sauce, or garlic aioli for dipping.

Per Serving: Calories: 218; Total Fat: 9g; Saturated Fat: 4g; Cholesterol: 71mg; Sodium: 552mg; Total Carbs: 23g; Dietary Fiber: 1g; Total Sugars: 1g; Protein: 12g

Spanish Fried Baby Squid

Servings: 2 | Prep Time: 10 Minutes | Cooking Time: 30 Minutes

Ingredients:

- 1 cup baby squid
- ½ cup semolina flour
- ½ tsp Spanish paprika
- ½ tsp garlic powder
- 2 eggs
- Salt and pepper to taste
- 2 tbsp lemon juice
- 1 tsp Old Bay seasoning

Directions:

1. Preheat air fryer to 180°C/350°F. Beat the eggs in a bowl. Stir in lemon juice and set aside.
2. Mix flour, Old Bay seasoning, garlic powder, paprika, salt, and pepper in another bowl.
3. Dip each piece of squid into the flour, then into the eggs, and then again into the flour. Transfer them to the greased frying basket and Air Fry for 18-20 minutes, shaking the basket occasionally until crispy and golden brown.
4. Serve hot.

Variations & Ingredients Tips:

- ▶ Serve with a dipping sauce, such as aioli or marinara sauce.
- ▶ Add some chopped fresh herbs, like parsley or cilantro, to the flour mixture for extra flavor.
- ▶ For a spicier version, increase the amount of paprika or add some cayenne pepper to the flour mixture.

Per Serving: Calories: 415; Total Fat: 8g; Saturated Fat: 2g; Cholesterol: 540mg; Sodium: 630mg; Total Carbs: 44g; Fiber: 3g; Sugars: 3g; Protein: 38g

Basil Feta Crostini

Servings: 4 | Prep Time: 5 Minutes | Cooking Time: 10 Minutes

Ingredients:

- 1 baguette, sliced
- ¼ cup olive oil
- 2 garlic cloves, minced
- 113 g feta cheese
- 2 tbsp basil, minced

Directions:

1. Preheat air fryer to 190°C/380°F. Combine together the olive oil and garlic in a bowl. Brush it over one side of each slice of bread. Put the bread in a single layer in the frying basket and Bake for 5 minutes. In a small bowl, mix together the feta cheese and basil. Remove the toast from the air fryer, then spread a thin layer of the feta cheese mixture over the top of each piece. Serve.

Variations & Ingredients Tips:

- ▶ Use goat cheese or ricotta instead of feta for a milder flavor.
- ▶ Top with diced tomatoes or roasted red peppers for added color and taste.
- ▶ Drizzle with balsamic glaze or honey before serving.

Per Serving: Calories: 364; Total Fat: 19g; Saturated Fat: 7g; Cholesterol: 33mg; Sodium: 674mg; Total Carbs: 38g; Dietary Fiber: 1g; Total Sugars: 1g; Protein: 11g

Vegetarian Fritters With Green Dip

Servings: 6 | Prep Time: 20 Minutes | Cooking Time: 40 Minutes

Ingredients:

- ½ cup grated carrots
- ½ cup grated zucchini
- ¼ cup minced yellow onion
- 1 garlic clove, minced
- 1 large egg
- ¼ cup flour
- ¼ cup bread crumbs
- Salt and pepper to taste
- ½ tsp ground cumin

- ½ avocado, peeled and pitted
- ½ cup plain Greek yogurt
- 1 tsp lime juice
- 1 tbsp white vinegar
- ¼ cup chopped cilantro

Directions:

1. Preheat air fryer to 190°C/375°F. Combine carrots, zucchini, onion, garlic, egg, flour, bread crumbs, salt, pepper, and cumin in a large bowl. Scoop out 12 equal portions of the vegetables and form them into patties. Arrange the patties on the greased basket. Air fry for 5 minutes, then flip the patties. Air fry for another 5 minutes. Check if the fritters are golden and cooked through. If more time is needed, cook for another 3-5 minutes. While the fritters are cooking, prepare the avocado sauce. Mash the avocado in a small bowl to the desired texture. Stir in yogurt, white vinegar, chopped cilantro, lime juice, and salt. When the fritter is done, transfer to a serving plate along with the avocado sauce for dipping. Serve warm and enjoy.

Variations & Ingredients Tips:

- Experiment with different vegetables like bell peppers, corn, or spinach in the fritter mixture.
- Add crumbled feta cheese or grated Parmesan to the batter for a cheesy flavor.
- Serve with tzatziki sauce, hummus, or sweet chili sauce for dipping variety.

Per Serving: Calories: 112; Total Fat: 5g; Saturated Fat: 1g; Cholesterol: 32mg; Sodium: 104mg; Total Carbohydrates: 13g; Dietary Fiber: 2g; Total Sugars: 2g; Protein: 4g

Barbecue Chicken Nachos

Servings: 3 | Prep Time: 10 Minutes | Cooking Time: 5 Minutes

Ingredients:

- 3 heaping cups (a little more than 85 g) Corn tortilla chips (gluten-free, if a concern)
- ¾ cup Shredded deboned and skinned rotisserie chicken meat (gluten-free, if a concern)
- 3 tablespoons Canned black beans, drained and rinsed
- 9 rings Pickled jalapeño slices
- 4 Small pickled cocktail onions, halved
- 3 tablespoons Barbecue sauce (any sort)
- ¾ cup (about 85 g) Shredded Cheddar cheese

Directions:

1. Preheat the air fryer to 200°C/400°F.
2. Cut a circle of parchment paper to line a 15 cm round cake pan for a small air fryer, an 18 cm round cake pan for a medium air fryer, or a 20 cm round cake pan for a large machine.
3. Fill the pan with an even layer of about two-thirds of the chips. Sprinkle the chicken evenly over the chips. Set the pan in the basket and air-fry undisturbed for 2 minutes.
4. Remove the basket from the machine. Scatter the beans, jalapeño rings, and pickled onion halves over the chicken. Drizzle the barbecue sauce over everything, then sprinkle the cheese on top.
5. Return the basket to the machine and air-fry undisturbed for 3 minutes, or until the cheese has melted and is bubbly. Remove the pan from the machine and cool for a couple of minutes before serving.

Variations & Ingredients Tips:

- Use pork carnitas or ground beef instead of chicken.
- Add sliced avocado or guacamole on top after cooking.
- Serve with sour cream, salsa and chopped cilantro.

Per Serving: Calories: 386; Total Fat: 20g; Saturated Fat: 9g; Cholesterol: 59mg; Sodium: 808mg; Total Carbs: 31g; Dietary Fiber: 5g; Total Sugars: 8g; Protein: 22g

Crispy Chicken Bites With Gorgonzola Sauce

Servings: 4 | Prep Time: 15 Minutes | Cooking Time: 30 Minutes

Ingredients:

- ¼ cup crumbled Gorgonzola cheese
- ¼ cup creamy blue cheese salad dressing
- 450 g chicken tenders, cut into thirds crosswise
- ½ cup sour cream
- 1 celery stalk, chopped
- 3 tbsp buffalo chicken sauce
- 1 cup panko bread crumbs
- 2 tbsp olive oil

Directions:

1. Preheat air fryer to 175°C/350°F. Blend together sour

cream, salad dressing, Gorgonzola cheese, and celery in a bowl. Set aside. Combine chicken pieces and Buffalo wing sauce in another bowl until the chicken is coated.
2. In a shallow bowl or pie plate, mix the bread crumbs and olive oil. Dip the chicken into the bread crumb mixture, patting the crumbs to keep them in place. Arrange the chicken in the greased frying basket and Air Fry for 8-9 minutes, shaking once halfway through cooking until the chicken is golden. Serve with the blue cheese sauce.

Variations & Ingredients Tips:

- Use boneless skinless chicken thighs instead of tenders.
- Substitute ranch dressing for the blue cheese dressing.
- Add some garlic powder or onion powder to the bread crumb mixture.

Per Serving: Calories: 446; Total Fat: 27g; Saturated Fat: 10g; Cholesterol: 92mg; Sodium: 815mg; Total Carbs: 19g; Dietary Fiber: 1g; Total Sugars: 3g; Protein: 32g

Crab Toasts

Servings: 15 | Prep Time: 10 Minutes | Cooking Time: 5 Minutes

Ingredients:

- 1 170 g can flaked crabmeat, well drained
- 3 tablespoons light mayonnaise
- ½ teaspoon lemon juice
- 1 teaspoon Worcestershire sauce
- ¼ cup shredded sharp Cheddar cheese
- ¼ cup shredded Parmesan cheese
- 1 loaf artisan bread, French bread, or baguette, cut into slices 10 mm thick

Directions:

1. Mix together all ingredients except the bread slices.
2. Spread each slice of bread with a thin layer of crabmeat mixture. (For a bread slice measuring 5 x 4 cm you will need about ½ tablespoon of crab mixture.)
3. Place in air fryer basket in single layer and cook at 180°C/360°F for 5 minutes or until tops brown and toast is crispy.
4. Repeat step 3 to cook remaining crab toasts.

Variations & Ingredients Tips:

- Use smoked salmon, cooked shrimp or lobster instead of crab.
- Add some minced jalapeños or hot sauce to the mixture for a spicy kick.
- Sprinkle with Old Bay seasoning or smoked paprika before cooking.

Per Serving: Calories: 104; Total Fat: 4g; Saturated Fat: 1g; Cholesterol: 17mg; Sodium: 271mg; Total Carbs: 12g; Dietary Fiber: 1g; Total Sugars: 1g; Protein: 5g

Sweet Potato Chips

Servings: 4 | Prep Time: 40 Minutes | Cooking Time: 10 Minutes

Ingredients:

- 2 medium sweet potatoes, washed
- 2 cups filtered water
- 1 tbsp avocado oil
- 2 tsp brown sugar
- ½ tsp salt

Directions:

1. Using a mandolin, slice the potatoes into 3-mm pieces. Add the water to a large bowl. Place the potatoes in the bowl, and soak for at least 30 minutes. Preheat the air fryer to 175°C/350°F. Drain the water and pat the chips dry with a paper towel or kitchen cloth. Toss the chips with the avocado oil, brown sugar, and salt. Liberally spray the air fryer basket with olive oil mist. Set the chips inside the air fryer, separating them so they're not on top of each other. Cook for 5 minutes, shake the basket, and cook another 5 minutes, or until browned. Remove and let cool a few minutes prior to serving. Repeat until all the chips are cooked.

Variations & Ingredients Tips:

- Use different types of potatoes like russet, Yukon Gold, or purple potatoes for varied flavors and colors.
- Season the chips with different spices like cinnamon, nutmeg, or pumpkin pie spice for a sweet twist.
- Serve with a dipping sauce like honey mustard, ranch, or garlic aioli.

Per Serving: Calories: 118; Total Fat: 4g; Saturated Fat: 1g; Sodium: 296mg; Total Carbohydrates: 20g; Dietary Fiber: 3g; Total Sugars: 6g; Protein: 1g

Rich Clam Spread

Servings: 6 | Prep Time: 15 Minutes | Cooking Time: 40 Minutes

Ingredients:

- 2 cans chopped clams in clam juice
- ⅓ cup panko bread crumbs
- 1 garlic clove, minced
- 1 tbsp olive oil
- 1 tbsp lemon juice
- ¼ tsp hot sauce
- 1 tsp Worcestershire sauce
- ½ tsp shallot powder
- ¼ tsp dried dill
- Salt and pepper to taste
- ½ tsp sweet paprika
- 4 tsp grated Parmesan cheese
- 2 celery stalks, chopped

Directions:

1. Completely drain one can of clams. Add them to a bowl along with the entire can of clams, breadcrumbs, garlic, olive oil, lemon juice, Worcestershire sauce, hot sauce, shallot powder, dill, pepper, salt, paprika, and 2 tbsp Parmesan. Combine well and set aside for 10 minutes. After that time, put the mixture in a greased baking dish. Preheat air fryer to 165°C/325°F. Put the dish in the air fryer and bake for 10 minutes. Sprinkle the remaining paprika and Parmesan, and continue to cook until golden brown on top, 8-10 minutes. Serve hot along with celery sticks.

Variations & Ingredients Tips:

- Add chopped bacon, sun-dried tomatoes, or artichoke hearts for extra flavor and texture.
- Serve with crackers, baguette slices, or pita chips for dipping.
- For a spicier version, increase the amount of hot sauce or add a pinch of cayenne pepper.

Per Serving: Calories: 99; Total Fat: 4g; Saturated Fat: 1g; Cholesterol: 16mg; Sodium: 312mg; Total Carbs: 8g; Dietary Fiber: 1g; Total Sugars: 1g; Protein: 7g

Wrapped Shrimp Bites

Servings: 4 | Prep Time: 5 Minutes | Cooking Time: 15 Minutes

Ingredients:

- 2 jumbo shrimp, peeled
- 2 bacon strips, sliced
- 2 tbsp lemon juice
- ½ tsp chipotle powder
- ½ tsp garlic salt

Directions:

1. Preheat air fryer to 175°C/350°F. Wrap the bacon around the shrimp and place the shrimp in the foil-lined frying basket, seam side down. Drizzle with lemon juice, chipotle powder and garlic salt. Air fry for 10 minutes, turning the shrimp once until cooked through and bacon is crispy. Serve hot.

Variations & Ingredients Tips:

- Use prosciutto, pancetta, or turkey bacon instead of regular bacon for a different flavor.
- Brush the wrapped shrimp with BBQ sauce, teriyaki sauce, or pesto before cooking for extra seasoning.
- Serve with cocktail sauce, remoulade, or mango salsa for dipping.

Per Serving: Calories: 59; Total Fat: 3g; Saturated Fat: 1g; Cholesterol: 55mg; Sodium: 619mg; Total Carbohydrates: 1g; Dietary Fiber: 0g; Total Sugars: 0g; Protein: 7g

Chicken Nachos

Servings: 6 | Prep Time: 10 Minutes | Cooking Time: 25 Minutes

Ingredients:

- 60 g baked corn tortilla chips
- 1 cup leftover roast chicken, shredded
- ½ cup canned black beans
- 1 red bell pepper, chopped
- ½ grated carrot
- 1 jalapeño pepper, minced
- 1/3 cup grated Swiss cheese
- 1 tomato, chopped

Directions:

1. Preheat air fryer to 180°C/360°F. Lay the tortilla chips in a single layer in a baking pan. Add the chicken, black beans, red bell pepper, carrot, jalapeño, and cheese on top. Bake in the air fryer for 9-12 minutes. Make sure the cheese melts and is slightly browned. Serve gar-

nished with tomatoes.

Variations & Ingredients Tips:

- Use pork carnitas or ground beef instead of chicken.
- Add sliced avocado, sour cream or salsa on top.
- Swap the Swiss cheese for pepper jack or a Mexican blend.

Per Serving: Calories: 173; Total Fat: 7g; Saturated Fat: 3g; Cholesterol: 30mg; Sodium: 269mg; Total Carbs: 16g; Dietary Fiber: 3g; Total Sugars: 2g; Protein: 12g

Fiery Sweet Chicken Wings

Servings: 4 | Prep Time: 10 Minutes | Cooking Time: 30 Minutes

Ingredients:

- 8 chicken wings
- 1 tbsp olive oil
- 3 tbsp brown sugar
- 2 tbsp maple syrup
- ½ cup apple cider vinegar
- ½ tsp Aleppo pepper flakes
- Salt to taste

Directions:

1. Preheat air fryer to 200°C/390°F. Toss the wings with olive oil in a bowl. Bake in the air fryer for 20 minutes, shaking the basket twice. While the chicken is cooking, whisk together sugar, maple syrup, vinegar, Aleppo pepper flakes, and salt in a small bowl. Transfer the wings to a baking pan, then pour the sauce over the wings. Toss well to coat. Cook in the air fryer until the wings are glazed, or for another 5 minutes. Serve hot.

Variations & Ingredients Tips:

- Use honey, agave or hot honey instead of maple syrup.
- Add some minced garlic, ginger or sriracha to the glaze.
- Sprinkle with sesame seeds or chopped scallions before serving.

Per Serving: Calories: 240; Total Fat: 12g; Saturated Fat: 3g; Cholesterol: 48mg; Sodium: 152mg; Total Carbs: 21; Dietary Fiber: 0g; Total Sugars: 19g; Protein: 12g

Poultry Recipes

Za'atar Chicken Drumsticks

Servings: 4 | Prep Time: 5 Minutes | Cooking Time: 45 Minutes

Ingredients:

- 2 tbsp butter, melted
- 8 chicken drumsticks
- 1 1/2 tbsp Za'atar seasoning
- Salt and pepper to taste
- 1 lemon, zested
- 2 tbsp parsley, chopped

Directions:

1. Preheat air fryer to 200°C/390°F.
2. Mix the Za'atar seasoning, lemon zest, parsley, salt, and pepper in a bowl. Add the chicken drumsticks and toss to coat.
3. Place them in the air fryer and brush them with butter.
4. Air Fry for 18-20 minutes, flipping once until crispy.
5. Serve and enjoy!

Variations & Ingredients Tips:

- Use chicken wings or thighs instead of drumsticks.
- Add sumac or sesame seeds to the spice mix.
- Squeeze fresh lemon juice over the drumsticks before serving.

Per Serving: Calories: 330; Total Fat: 21g; Saturated Fat:

8g; Cholesterol: 175mg; Sodium: 460mg; Total Carbs: 1g; Dietary Fiber: 1g; Total Sugars: 0g; Protein: 31g

Crispy Duck With Cherry Sauce

Servings: 2 | Prep Time: 20 Minutes | Cooking Time: 33 Minutes

Ingredients:

- 1 whole duck (up to 2.3 kg), split in half, back and rib bones removed
- 1 teaspoon olive oil
- salt and freshly ground black pepper
- Cherry Sauce:
- 1 tablespoon butter
- 1 shallot, minced
- ½ cup sherry
- ¾ cup cherry preserves
- 1 cup chicken stock
- 1 teaspoon white wine vinegar
- 1 teaspoon fresh thyme leaves
- salt and freshly ground black pepper

Directions:

1. Preheat the air fryer to 200°C/400°F.
2. Trim some of the fat from the duck. Rub olive oil on the duck and season with salt and pepper. Place the duck halves in the air fryer basket, breast side up and facing the center of the basket.
3. Air-fry the duck for 20 minutes. Turn the duck over and air-fry for another 6 minutes.
4. While duck is air-frying, make the cherry sauce. Melt the butter in a large sauté pan. Add the shallot and sauté until it is just starting to brown – about 2 to 3 minutes. Add the sherry and deglaze the pan by scraping up any brown bits from the bottom of the pan. Simmer the liquid for a few minutes, until it has reduced by half. Add the cherry preserves, chicken stock and white wine vinegar. Whisk well to combine all the ingredients. Simmer the sauce until it thickens and coats the back of a spoon – about 5 to 7 minutes. Season with salt and pepper and stir in the fresh thyme leaves.
5. When the air fryer timer goes off, spoon some cherry sauce over the duck and continue to air-fry at 200°C/400°F for 4 more minutes. Then, turn the duck halves back over so that the breast side is facing up. Spoon more cherry sauce over the top of the duck, covering the skin completely. Air-fry for 3 more minutes and then remove the duck to a plate to rest for a few minutes.
6. Serve the duck in halves, or cut each piece in half again for a smaller serving. Spoon any additional sauce over the duck or serve it on the side.

Variations & Ingredients Tips:

- ▸ Use duck breasts or legs instead of a whole duck for quicker cooking time.
- ▸ Substitute cherry preserves with blackberry, raspberry, or apricot jam.
- ▸ Garnish with fresh herbs like rosemary, sage, or parsley before serving.

Per Serving: Calories: 610; Total Fat: 36g; Saturated Fat: 12g; Sodium: 430mg; Total Carbohydrates: 41g; Dietary Fiber: 1g; Total Sugars: 34g; Protein: 34g

Fiesta Chicken Plate

Servings: 4 | Prep Time: 10 Minutes | Cooking Time: 15 Minutes

Ingredients:

- 450g boneless, skinless chicken breasts (2 large breasts)
- 2 tablespoons lime juice
- 1 teaspoon cumin
- 1/2 teaspoon salt
- 1/2 cup grated Pepper Jack cheese
- 1 (450g) can refried beans
- 1/2 cup salsa
- 2 cups shredded lettuce
- 1 medium tomato, chopped
- 2 avocados, peeled and sliced
- 1 small onion, sliced into thin rings
- Sour cream
- Tortilla chips (optional)

Directions:

1. Split each chicken breast in half lengthwise.
2. Mix lime juice, cumin, and salt together and brush on all surfaces of chicken breasts.
3. Place in air fryer basket and cook at 200°C/390°F for 15 minutes, until well done.
4. Divide the cheese evenly over chicken breasts and cook for an additional minute to melt cheese.
5. While chicken is cooking, heat refried beans on stovetop or in microwave.
6. When ready to serve, divide beans among 4 plates. Place chicken breasts on top of beans and spoon salsa over. Arrange the lettuce, tomatoes, and avocados art-

fully on each plate and scatter with the onion rings.
7. Pass sour cream at the table and serve with tortilla chips if desired.

Variations & Ingredients Tips:

- Substitute Pepper Jack with Monterey Jack or cheddar cheese.
- Add some pickled jalapeños or hot sauce for extra spice.
- Use black beans instead of refried for more texture.

Per Serving: Calories: 550; Total Fat: 32g; Saturated Fat: 8g; Cholesterol: 105mg; Sodium: 920mg; Total Carbs: 35g; Dietary Fiber: 12g; Total Sugars: 4g; Protein: 38g

Chicken Cordon Bleu Patties

Servings: 4 | Prep Time: 15 Minutes | Cooking Time: 30 Minutes

Ingredients:

- 1/3 cup grated Fontina cheese
- 3 tbsp milk
- 1/3 cup bread crumbs
- 1 egg, beaten
- 1/2 tsp dried parsley
- Salt and pepper to taste
- 565g ground chicken
- ¼ cup finely chopped ham

Directions:

1. Preheat air fryer to 175°C/350°F.
2. Mix milk, breadcrumbs, egg, parsley, salt and pepper in a bowl.
3. Using hands, add chicken and gently mix until just combined.
4. Divide into 8 portions and shape into thin patties on waxed paper.
5. On 4 patties, top with ham and Fontina cheese, then place another patty on top.
6. Pinch edges together to seal in filling.
7. Arrange patties in greased air fryer basket and cook for 14-16 minutes until cooked through.
8. Serve and enjoy!

Variations & Ingredients Tips:

- Use different cheese like swiss or cheddar.
- Add mushrooms or spinach to the filling.
- Serve with a mustard or garlic aioli sauce for dipping.

Per Serving: Calories: 368; Total Fat: 14g; Saturated Fat: 5g; Cholesterol: 197mg; Sodium: 536mg; Total Carbs: 17g; Dietary Fiber: 1g; Total Sugars: 1g; Protein: 43g

Moroccan-style Chicken Strips

Servings: 4 | Prep Time: 10 Minutes | Cooking Time: 30 Minutes

Ingredients:

- 4 chicken breasts, cut into strips
- 2 tsp olive oil
- 2 tbsp cornstarch
- 3 garlic cloves, minced
- 1/2 cup chicken broth
- 1/4 cup lemon juice
- 1 tbsp honey
- 1/2 tsp ras el hanout
- 1 cup cooked couscous

Directions:

1. Preheat air fryer to 200°C/400°F.
2. Mix the chicken and olive oil in a bowl, then add the cornstarch. Stir to coat. Add the garlic and transfer to a baking pan. Put the pan in the fryer. Bake for 10 minutes. Stir at least once during cooking.
3. When done, pour in the chicken broth, lemon juice, honey, and ras el hanout. Bake for an additional 6-9 minutes or until the sauce is thick and the chicken cooked through with no pink showing.
4. Serve with couscous.

Variations & Ingredients Tips:

- Substitute ras el hanout with a blend of cumin, paprika, cinnamon and ginger.
- Add some diced dried apricots or golden raisins to the sauce.
- Garnish with chopped fresh cilantro and toasted almonds.

Per Serving: Calories: 280; Total Fat: 6g; Saturated Fat: 1g; Cholesterol: 110mg; Sodium: 220mg; Total Carbs: 21g; Dietary Fiber: 1g; Total Sugars: 7g; Protein: 36g

Spicy Black Bean Turkey Burgers With Cumin-avocado Spread

Servings: 2 | Prep Time: 10 Minutes | Cooking Time: 20 Minutes

Ingredients:

- 1 cup canned black beans, drained and rinsed
- 340g lean ground turkey
- 2 tablespoons minced red onion
- 1 Jalapeño pepper, seeded and minced
- 2 tablespoons plain breadcrumbs
- 1/2 teaspoon chili powder
- 1/4 teaspoon cayenne pepper
- Salt, to taste
- Olive or vegetable oil
- 2 slices pepper jack cheese
- Toasted burger rolls, sliced tomatoes, lettuce leaves
- Cumin-Avocado Spread:
- 1 ripe avocado
- Juice of 1 lime
- 1 teaspoon ground cumin
- 1/2 teaspoon salt
- 1 tablespoon chopped fresh cilantro
- Freshly ground black pepper

Directions:

1. Place the black beans in a large bowl and smash them slightly with the back of a fork. Add the ground turkey, red onion, Jalapeño pepper, breadcrumbs, chili powder and cayenne pepper. Season with salt. Mix with your hands to combine all the ingredients and then shape them into 2 patties. Brush both sides of the burger patties with a little olive or vegetable oil.
2. Preheat the air fryer to 190°C/380°F.
3. Transfer the burgers to the air fryer basket and air-fry for 20 minutes, flipping them over halfway through the cooking process. Top the burgers with the pepper jack cheese (securing the slices to the burgers with a toothpick) for the last 2 minutes of the cooking process.
4. While the burgers are cooking, make the cumin avocado spread. Place the avocado, lime juice, cumin and salt in food processor and process until smooth. (For a chunkier spread, you can mash this by hand in a bowl.) Stir in the cilantro and season with freshly ground black pepper. Chill the spread until you are ready to serve.
5. When the burgers have finished cooking, remove them from the air fryer and let them rest on a plate, covered gently with aluminum foil. Brush a little olive oil on the insides of the burger rolls. Place the rolls, cut side up, into the air fryer basket and air-fry at 200°C/400°F for 1 minute to toast and warm them.
6. Spread the cumin-avocado spread on the rolls and build your burgers with lettuce and sliced tomatoes and any other ingredient you like. Serve warm with a side of sweet potato fries.

Variations & Ingredients Tips:

- Use black bean veggie patties instead of turkey for a vegetarian option.
- Add crumbled feta or shredded cheddar to the burger patty mixture.
- Serve on whole wheat buns or lettuce wraps.

Per Serving (1 burger + spread): Calories: 566; Total Fat: 24g; Saturated Fat: 6g; Cholesterol: 115mg; Sodium: 647mg; Total Carbs: 46g; Dietary Fiber: 14g; Total Sugars: 4g; Protein: 43g

Pickle Brined Fried Chicken

Servings: 4 | Prep Time: 20 Minutes (plus Brining Time) | Cooking Time: 47 Minutes

Ingredients:

- 4 bone-in, skin-on chicken legs, cut into drumsticks and thighs (about 1.6kg)
- Pickle juice from a 680g jar of kosher dill pickles
- 1/2 cup flour
- Salt and freshly ground black pepper
- 2 eggs
- 1 cup fine breadcrumbs
- 1 teaspoon salt
- 1 teaspoon freshly ground black pepper
- 1/2 teaspoon ground paprika
- 1/8 teaspoon ground cayenne pepper
- Vegetable or canola oil in a spray bottle

Directions:

1. Place the chicken in a shallow dish and pour the pickle juice over the top. Cover and transfer the chicken to the refrigerator to brine in the pickle juice for 3 to 8 hours.
2. When you are ready to cook, remove the chicken from the refrigerator to let it come to room temperature while you set up a dredging station. Place the flour in a shallow dish and season well with salt and freshly ground black pepper. Whisk the eggs in a second shallow dish. In a third shallow dish, combine the breadcrumbs, salt, pepper, paprika and cayenne pepper.
3. Preheat the air fryer to 190°C/370°F.
4. Remove the chicken from the pickle brine and gently dry it with a clean kitchen towel. Dredge each piece of chicken in the flour, then dip it into the egg mixture,

and finally press it into the breadcrumb mixture to coat all sides of the chicken. Place the breaded chicken on a plate or baking sheet and spray each piece all over with vegetable oil.
5. Air-fry the chicken in two batches. Place two chicken thighs and two drumsticks into the air fryer basket. Air-fry for 10 minutes. Then, gently turn the chicken pieces over and air-fry for another 10 minutes. Remove the chicken pieces and let them rest on plate – do not cover. Repeat with the second batch of chicken, air-frying for 20 minutes, turning the chicken over halfway through.
6. Lower the temperature of the air fryer to 170°C/340°F. Place the first batch of chicken on top of the second batch already in the basket and air-fry for an additional 7 minutes.
7. Serve warm and enjoy.

Variations & Ingredients Tips:

- Use buttermilk instead of pickle juice for a traditional fried chicken brine.
- Add dried herbs like thyme, oregano or rosemary to the breading mix.
- Serve with hot sauce, honey or ranch dressing for dipping.

Per Serving: Calories: 620; Total Fat: 33g; Saturated Fat: 9g; Cholesterol: 295mg; Sodium: 2020mg; Total Carbs: 23g; Dietary Fiber: 1g; Total Sugars: 2g; Protein: 58g

Chicken Flautas

Servings: 6 | Prep Time: 15 Minutes | Cooking Time: 8 Minutes

Ingredients:

- 6 tablespoons whipped cream cheese
- 1 cup shredded cooked chicken
- 6 tablespoons mild pico de gallo salsa
- 1/3 cup shredded Mexican cheese
- 1/2 teaspoon taco seasoning
- Six 20-cm flour tortillas
- 2 cups shredded lettuce
- 1/2 cup guacamole

Directions:

1. Preheat the air fryer to 190°C/370°F.
2. In a bowl, mix the cream cheese, chicken, salsa, shredded cheese, and taco seasoning.
3. Lay the tortillas out and divide the chicken mixture evenly among them, leaving 2.5-cm from edges.
4. Spray basket with oil. Roll up flautas and place seam-side down in basket. Mist tops with oil.
5. Cook in batches if needed, for 7 minutes until browned.
6. Serve warm over shredded lettuce with guacamole on top.

Variations & Ingredients Tips:

- Use corn tortillas instead of flour for a crispier texture.
- Add refried beans or Mexican rice as a side.
- Top with crumbled queso fresco or pico de gallo.

Per Serving (2 flautas): Calories: 313; Total Fat: 17g; Saturated Fat: 6g; Cholesterol: 54mg; Sodium: 652mg; Total Carbs: 26g; Dietary Fiber: 3g; Total Sugars: 2g; Protein: 15g

Chicken Salad With White Dressing

Servings: 2 | Prep Time: 15 Minutes | Cooking Time: 20 Minutes

Ingredients:

- 2 chicken breasts, cut into strips
- ¼ cup diced peeled red onion
- ½ peeled English cucumber, diced
- 1 tbsp crushed red pepper flakes
- 1 cup Greek yogurt
- 3 tbsp light mayonnaise
- 1 tbsp mustard
- 1 tsp chopped dill
- 1 tsp chopped mint
- 1 tsp lemon juice
- 2 cloves garlic, minced
- Salt and pepper to taste
- 3 cups mixed greens
- 10 Kalamata olives, halved
- 1 tomato, diced
- ¼ cup feta cheese crumbles

Directions:

1. Preheat air fryer at 180°C/350°F.
2. In a small bowl, whisk the Greek yogurt, mayonnaise, mustard, cucumber, dill, mint, salt, lemon juice, and garlic, and let chill the resulting dressing covered in the fridge until ready to use.
3. Sprinkle the chicken strips with salt and pepper. Place them in the air fryer basket and Air Fry for 10 minutes,

tossing once.

4. Place the mixed greens and pepper flakes in a salad bowl. Top each with red onion, olives, tomato, feta cheese, and grilled chicken.
5. Drizzle with the dressing and serve.

Variations & Ingredients Tips:

- Use romaine lettuce, spinach, or arugula instead of mixed greens.
- Add sliced bell peppers, carrots, or radishes for extra crunch.
- Substitute feta with goat cheese or shaved Parmesan.

Per Serving: Calories: 520; Total Fat: 27g; Saturated Fat: 8g; Sodium: 1120mg; Total Carbohydrates: 18g; Dietary Fiber: 5g; Total Sugars: 9g; Protein: 52g

Mom's Chicken Wings

Servings: 4 | Prep Time: 10 Minutes | Cooking Time: 35 Minutes

Ingredients:

- 900g chicken wings, split at the joint
- 1 tbsp water
- 1 tbsp sesame oil
- 2 tbsp Dijon mustard
- 1/4 tsp chili powder
- 1 tbsp tamari
- 1 tsp honey
- 1 tsp white wine vinegar

Directions:

1. Preheat air fryer to 200°C/400°F.
2. Coat the wings with sesame oil. Place them in the frying basket and Air Fry for 16-18 minutes, tossing once or twice.
3. Whisk the remaining ingredients in a bowl. Reserve.
4. When ready, transfer the wings to a serving bowl. Pour the previously prepared sauce over and toss to coat.
5. Serve immediately.

Variations & Ingredients Tips:

- Add minced garlic and grated ginger to the sauce.
- Sprinkle wings with toasted sesame seeds before serving.
- Serve with crisp cucumber sticks and extra sauce for dipping.

Per Serving: Calories: 420; Total Fat: 30g; Saturated Fat: 8g; Cholesterol: 125mg; Sodium: 740mg; Total Carbs: 5g; Dietary Fiber: 0g; Total Sugars: 3g; Protein: 31g

Chicken Fried Steak With Gravy

Servings: 4 | Prep Time: 15 Minutes | Cooking Time: 10 Minutes Per Batch

Ingredients:

- 1/2 cup flour
- 2 teaspoons salt, divided
- Freshly ground black pepper
- 1/4 teaspoon garlic powder
- 1 cup buttermilk
- 1 cup fine breadcrumbs
- 4 tenderized top round steaks (about 170-225g each; 1.3cm thick)
- Vegetable or canola oil
- For the Gravy:
- 2 tablespoons butter or bacon drippings
- 1/4 onion, minced (about 1/4 cup)
- 1 clove garlic, smashed
- 1/4 teaspoon dried thyme
- 3 tablespoons flour
- 1 cup milk
- Salt and lots of freshly ground black pepper
- A few dashes of Worcestershire sauce

Directions:

1. Set up a dredging station: flour+1 tsp salt+pepper+garlic powder in one bowl, buttermilk in second, breadcrumbs+1 tsp salt in third.
2. Dip steaks in flour, buttermilk, then breadcrumbs, pressing to adhere. Place on baking sheet and spray both sides generously with oil.
3. Preheat air fryer to 205°C/400°F.
4. Air fry steaks in batches for 10 mins, flipping halfway through. Hold first batch warm at 75°C/170°F.
5. Make gravy: Melt butter, cook onion, garlic, thyme 5 mins. Stir in flour 5 more mins. Whisk in milk and boil until thickened. Season with salt, pepper, Worcestershire.
6. Serve steaks with gravy, mashed potatoes and veggies.

Variations & Ingredients Tips:

- Use chicken breast or pork chops instead of steak.
- Add cayenne or paprika to the breading for spice.
- Use chicken or veggie broth instead of milk for the gravy.

Per Serving (1 steak + gravy): Calories: 592; Total Fat: 27g; Saturated Fat: 10g; Cholesterol: 133mg; Sodium: 1095mg; Total Carbs: 49g; Dietary Fiber: 2g; Total Sugars: 4g; Protein: 35g

Nashville Hot Chicken

Servings: 4 | Prep Time: 20 Minutes | Cooking Time: 27 Minutes

Ingredients:

- 1 (1.8kg) chicken, cut into 6 pieces (2 breasts, 2 thighs and 2 drumsticks)
- 2 eggs
- 1 cup buttermilk
- 2 cups all-purpose flour
- 2 tablespoons paprika
- 1 teaspoon garlic powder
- 1 teaspoon onion powder
- 2 teaspoons salt
- 1 teaspoon freshly ground black pepper
- Vegetable oil, in a spray bottle
- Nashville Hot Sauce:
- 1 tablespoon cayenne pepper
- 1 teaspoon salt
- 1/4 cup vegetable oil
- 4 slices white bread
- Dill pickle slices

Directions:

1. Cut the chicken breasts into 2 pieces so that you have a total of 8 pieces of chicken.
2. Set up a two-stage dredging station. Whisk the eggs and buttermilk together in a bowl. Combine the flour, paprika, garlic powder, onion powder, salt and black pepper in a zipper-sealable plastic bag. Dip the chicken pieces into the egg-buttermilk mixture, then toss them in the seasoned flour, coating all sides. Repeat this procedure (egg mixture and then flour mixture) one more time. This can be a little messy, but make sure all sides of the chicken are completely covered. Spray the chicken with vegetable oil and set aside.
3. Preheat the air fryer to 190°C/370°F. Spray or brush the bottom of the air-fryer basket with a little vegetable oil.
4. Air-fry the chicken in two batches at 190°C/370°F for 20 minutes, flipping the pieces over halfway through the cooking process. Transfer the chicken to a plate, but do not cover. Repeat with the second batch of chicken.
5. Lower the temperature on the air fryer to 170°C/340°F. Flip the chicken back over and place the first batch of chicken on top of the second batch already in the basket. Air-fry for another 7 minutes.
6. While the chicken is air-frying, combine the cayenne pepper and salt in a bowl. Heat the vegetable oil in a small saucepan and when it is very hot, add it to the spice mix, whisking until smooth. It will sizzle briefly when you add it to the spices.
7. Place the fried chicken on top of the white bread slices and brush the hot sauce all over chicken. Top with the pickle slices and serve warm. Enjoy the heat and the flavor!

Variations & Ingredients Tips:

- Adjust the cayenne to your spice preference.
- Use chicken tenders for easier prep and cooking.
- Serve in a sandwich with coleslaw and comeback sauce.

Per Serving: Calories: 860; Total Fat: 58g; Saturated Fat: 12g; Cholesterol: 290mg; Sodium: 2210mg; Total Carbs: 36g; Dietary Fiber: 2g; Total Sugars: 5g; Protein: 55g

Guajillo Chile Chicken Meatballs

Servings: 4 | Prep Time: 10 Minutes | Cooking Time: 30 Minutes

Ingredients:

- 450g ground chicken
- 1 large egg
- 1/2 cup bread crumbs
- 1 tbsp sour cream
- 2 tsp brown mustard
- 2 tbsp grated onion
- 2 tbsp tomato paste
- 1 tsp ground cumin
- 1 tsp guajillo chile powder
- 2 tbsp olive oil

Directions:

1. Preheat air fryer to 175°C/350°F.
2. Mix the ground chicken, egg, bread crumbs, sour cream, mustard, onion, tomato paste, cumin, and chili powder in a bowl. Form into 16 meatballs.
3. Place the meatballs in the greased frying basket and Air Fry for 8-10 minutes, shaking once until browned and cooked through.
4. Serve immediately.

Variations & Ingredients Tips:

- Use ground turkey for a leaner option.
- Add some minced garlic or cilantro to the mix.
- Serve with salsa, guacamole or queso fresco.

Per Serving: Calories: 330; Total Fat: 22g; Saturated Fat: 5g; Cholesterol: 165mg; Sodium: 270mg; Total Carbs: 7g; Dietary Fiber: 1g; Total Sugars: 2g; Protein: 27g

Chicken Schnitzel Dogs

Servings: 4 | Prep Time: 20 Minutes | Cooking Time: 10 Minutes

Ingredients:

- ½ cup flour
- ½ teaspoon salt
- 1 teaspoon marjoram
- 1 teaspoon dried parsley flakes
- ½ teaspoon thyme
- 1 egg
- 1 teaspoon lemon juice
- 1 teaspoon water
- 1 cup breadcrumbs
- 4 chicken tenders, pounded thin
- oil for misting or cooking spray
- 4 whole-grain hotdog buns
- 4 slices Gouda cheese
- 1 small Granny Smith apple, thinly sliced
- ½ cup shredded Napa cabbage
- coleslaw dressing

Directions:

1. In a shallow dish, mix together the flour, salt, marjoram, parsley, and thyme.
2. In another shallow dish, beat together egg, lemon juice, and water.
3. Place breadcrumbs in a third shallow dish.
4. Cut each of the flattened chicken tenders in half lengthwise.
5. Dip flattened chicken strips in flour mixture, then egg wash. Let excess egg drip off and roll in breadcrumbs. Spray both sides with oil or cooking spray.
6. Cook at 200°C/390°F for 5 minutes. Spray with oil, turn over, and spray other side.
7. Cook for 3 to 5 minutes more, until well done and crispy brown.
8. To serve, place 2 schnitzel strips on bottom of each hot dog bun. Top with cheese, sliced apple, and cabbage. Drizzle with coleslaw dressing and top with other half of bun.

Variations & Ingredients Tips:

- Use turkey or pork cutlets instead of chicken for different schnitzel options.
- Add sauerkraut, pickles, or mustard for German-style toppings.
- Serve with a side of potato salad or French fries.

Per Serving: Calories: 480; Total Fat: 20g; Saturated Fat: 6g; Sodium: 1020mg; Total Carbohydrates: 48g; Dietary Fiber: 6g; Total Sugars: 9g; Protein: 31g

Sweet Chili Spiced Chicken

Servings: 4 | Prep Time: 10 Minutes | Cooking Time: 43 Minutes

Ingredients:

- 2 tablespoons brown sugar
- 2 tablespoons paprika
- 1 teaspoon dry mustard powder
- 1 teaspoon chili powder
- 2 tablespoons coarse sea salt or kosher salt
- 2 teaspoons coarsely ground black pepper
- 1 tablespoon vegetable oil
- 1 (1.6kg) chicken, cut into 8 pieces

Directions:

1. Make spice rub by combining brown sugar, paprika, mustard, chili powder, salt and pepper.
2. Rub oil over chicken pieces then rub spice mix onto chicken to coat completely.
3. Preheat air fryer to 190°C/370°F.
4. Air fry chicken in 2 batches: thighs and drumsticks first for 10 mins per side.
5. Then breasts for 8 mins skin-side down, flip and cook 12 more mins.
6. Lower heat to 170°C/340°F. Stack chicken and air fry 3 more mins.
7. Let rest 5 mins before serving.

Variations & Ingredients Tips:

- Use chicken thighs only if desired.
- Add cayenne pepper or chipotle powder for extra heat.
- Marinate chicken in spice rub up to 24 hours before cooking.

Per Serving (2 pieces): Calories: 512; Total Fat: 24g;

Saturated Fat: 6g; Cholesterol: 199mg; Sodium: 2718mg; Total Carbs: 8g; Dietary Fiber: 2g; Total Sugars: 4g; Protein: 61g

Asian-style Orange Chicken

Servings: 4 | Prep Time: 15 Minutes | Cooking Time: 25 Minutes

Ingredients:

- 454 grams chicken breasts, cubed
- Salt and pepper to taste
- 6 tbsp cornstarch
- 1 cup orange juice
- ¼ cup orange marmalade
- ¼ cup ketchup
- ½ tsp ground ginger
- 2 tbsp soy sauce
- 1 1/3 cups edamame beans

Directions:

1. Preheat the air fryer to 190°C/375°F.
2. Sprinkle the chicken cubes with salt and pepper. Coat with 4 tbsp of cornstarch and set aside on a wire rack.
3. Mix the orange juice, marmalade, ketchup, ginger, soy sauce, and the remaining cornstarch in a cake pan, then stir in the beans.
4. Set the pan in the air fryer basket and Bake for 5-8 minutes, stirring once during cooking until the sauce is thick and bubbling. Remove from the fryer and set aside.
5. Put the chicken in the air fryer basket and fry for 10-12 minutes, shaking the basket once.
6. Stir the chicken into the sauce and beans in the pan. Return to the fryer and reheat for 2 minutes.

Variations & Ingredients Tips:

- Substitute chicken with tofu or shrimp for different protein options.
- Add sliced bell peppers, carrots, or broccoli to the sauce for extra veggies.
- Serve over steamed rice, quinoa, or noodles for a complete meal.

Per Serving: Calories: 400; Total Fat: 6g; Saturated Fat: 1g; Sodium: 830mg; Total Carbohydrates: 52g; Dietary Fiber: 5g; Total Sugars: 25g; Protein: 34g

Fiery Chicken Meatballs

Servings: 4 | Prep Time: 15 Minutes | Cooking Time: 20 Minutes + Chilling Time

Ingredients:

- 2 jalapeños, seeded and diced
- 2 tbsp shredded Cheddar cheese
- 1 tsp Quick Pickled Jalapeños
- 2 tbsp white wine vinegar
- 1/2 tsp granulated sugar
- Salt and pepper to taste
- 1 tbsp ricotta cheese
- 340g ground chicken
- 1/4 tsp smoked paprika
- 1 tsp garlic powder
- 1 cup bread crumbs
- 1/4 tsp salt

Directions:

1. Combine the jalapeños, white wine vinegar, sugar, black pepper, and salt in a bowl. Let sit the jalapeño mixture in the fridge for 15 minutes.
2. In a bowl, combine ricotta cheese, cheddar cheese, and 1 tsp of the jalapeños. Form mixture into 8 balls.
3. Mix the ground chicken, smoked paprika, garlic powder, and salt in a bowl. Form mixture into 8 meatballs. Form a hole in the chicken meatballs, press a cheese ball into the hole and form chicken around the cheese ball, sealing the cheese ball in meatballs.
4. Preheat air fryer at 175°C/350°F. Mix the breadcrumbs and salt in a bowl. Roll stuffed meatballs in the mixture. Place the meatballs in the greased frying basket. Air Fry for 10 minutes, turning once.
5. Serve immediately.

Variations & Ingredients Tips:

- Use diced pickled jalapeños instead of fresh for a milder heat.
- Mix some chopped cilantro or parsley into the chicken.
- Serve with ranch or blue cheese dressing for dipping.

Per Serving: Calories: 270; Total Fat: 13g; Saturated Fat: 5g; Cholesterol: 115mg; Sodium: 610mg; Total Carbs: 14g; Dietary Fiber: 1g; Total Sugars: 2g; Protein: 24g

Teriyaki Chicken Legs

Servings: 2 | Prep Time: 5 Minutes | Cooking Time: 20 Minutes

Ingredients:

- 4 tablespoons teriyaki sauce
- 1 tablespoon orange juice
- 1 teaspoon smoked paprika
- 4 chicken legs
- Cooking spray

Directions:

1. Mix together teriyaki sauce, orange juice and smoked paprika.
2. Brush sauce mixture on all sides of chicken legs.
3. Spray air fryer basket with cooking spray and add chicken legs.
4. Cook at 180°C/360°F for 6 mins. Turn and baste with sauce.
5. Cook 6 more mins, turn and baste again.
6. Cook 8 additional mins until juices run clear when pierced.

Variations & Ingredients Tips:

▶ Use chicken thighs or drumsticks instead of whole legs.
▶ Add garlic powder, ginger or honey to the teriyaki sauce.
▶ Brush with extra sauce after cooking and broil 2-3 mins for caramelization.

Per Serving (2 legs): Calories: 383; Total Fat: 18g; Saturated Fat: 4g; Cholesterol: 194mg; Sodium: 1096mg; Total Carbs: 15g; Dietary Fiber: 0g; Total Sugars: 10g; Protein: 41g

Lemon Herb Whole Cornish Hen

Servings: 2 | Prep Time: 15 Minutes | Cooking Time: 50 Minutes

Ingredients:

- 1 Cornish hen
- 1/4 cup olive oil
- 2 tbsp lemon juice
- 2 tbsp sage, chopped
- 2 tbsp thyme, chopped
- 4 garlic cloves, chopped
- Salt and pepper to taste
- 1 celery stalk, chopped
- 1/2 small onion
- 1/2 lemon, juiced and zested
- 2 tbsp chopped parsley

Directions:

1. Preheat air fryer to 190°C/380°F.
2. Whisk the olive oil, lemon juice, sage, thyme, garlic, salt, and pepper in a bowl. Rub the mixture on the tops and sides of the hen. Pour any excess inside the cavity of the bird.
3. Stuff the celery, onion, and lemon juice and zest into the cavity of the hen.
4. Put in the frying basket and Roast for 40-45 minutes.
5. Cut the hen in half and serve garnished with parsley.

Variations & Ingredients Tips:

▶ Use orange juice and zest for a different citrus flavor.
▶ Add sliced garlic and butter under the skin before cooking.
▶ Serve with roasted potatoes and a green salad.

Per Serving: Calories: 720; Total Fat: 55g; Saturated Fat: 13g; Cholesterol: 255mg; Sodium: 340mg; Total Carbs: 7g; Dietary Fiber: 2g; Total Sugars: 2g; Protein: 51g

Poblano Bake

Servings: 4 | Prep Time: 15 Minutes | Cooking Time: 11 Minutes Per Batch

Ingredients:

- 2 large poblano peppers (approx. 14 cm long excluding stem)
- 340g ground turkey, raw
- 3/4 cup cooked brown rice
- 1 teaspoon chile powder
- 1/2 teaspoon ground cumin
- 1/2 teaspoon garlic powder
- 115g sharp Cheddar cheese, grated
- 1 (225g) jar salsa, warmed

Directions:

1. Slice each pepper in half lengthwise so that you have four wide, flat pepper halves.
2. Remove seeds and membrane and discard. Rinse inside and out.
3. In a large bowl, combine turkey, rice, chile powder, cumin, and garlic powder. Mix well.
4. Divide turkey filling into 4 portions and stuff one into

each of the 4 pepper halves. Press lightly to pack down.
5. Place 2 pepper halves in air fryer basket and cook at 200°C/390°F for 10 minutes or until turkey is well done.
6. Top each pepper half with 1/4 of the grated cheese. Cook 1 more minute or just until cheese melts.
7. Repeat steps 5 and 6 to cook remaining pepper halves.
8. To serve, place each pepper half on a plate and top with 60 ml/1/4 cup warm salsa.

Variations & Ingredients Tips:

- Use ground beef or chicken instead of turkey.
- Add some cooked black beans or corn to the filling.
- Top with sliced avocado, sour cream or chopped cilantro.

Per Serving: Calories: 340; Total Fat: 19g; Saturated Fat: 8g; Cholesterol: 105mg; Sodium: 660mg; Total Carbs: 15g; Dietary Fiber: 2g; Total Sugars: 3g; Protein: 29g

Bacon & Chicken Flatbread

Servings: 2 | Prep Time: 20 Minutes | Cooking Time: 35 Minutes

Ingredients:

- 1 flatbread dough
- 1 chicken breast, cubed
- 1 cup breadcrumbs
- 2 eggs, beaten
- Salt and pepper to taste
- 2 tsp dry rosemary
- 1 tsp fajita seasoning
- 1 tsp onion powder
- 3 bacon strips
- ½ tbsp ranch sauce

Directions:

1. Preheat air fryer to 180°C/360°F.
2. Place the breadcrumbs, onion powder, rosemary, salt, and pepper in a mixing bowl. Coat the chicken with the mixture, dip into the beaten eggs, then roll again into the dry ingredients.
3. Arrange the coated chicken pieces on one side of the greased air fryer basket. On the other side of the basket, lay the bacon strips.
4. Air Fry for 6 minutes. Turn the bacon pieces over and flip the chicken and cook for another 6 minutes.
5. Roll the flatbread out and spread the ranch sauce all over the surface. Top with the bacon and chicken and sprinkle with fajita seasoning.
6. Close the bread to contain the filling and place it in the air fryer. Cook for 10 minutes, flipping the flatbread once until golden brown.
7. Let it cool for a few minutes. Then slice and serve.

Variations & Ingredients Tips:

- Use turkey bacon or prosciutto instead of regular bacon for a leaner option.
- Add sliced avocado, tomatoes, or lettuce to the flatbread for extra veggies.
- Substitute ranch sauce with BBQ sauce, honey mustard, or hot sauce for different flavors.

Per Serving: Calories: 580; Total Fat: 23g; Saturated Fat: 6g; Sodium: 1180mg; Total Carbohydrates: 58g; Dietary Fiber: 3g; Total Sugars: 4g; Protein: 38g

Beef, Pork & Lamb Recipes

Greek Pork Chops

Servings: 4 | Prep Time: 10 Minutes | Cooking Time: 30 Minutes

Ingredients:

- 3 tbsp grated Halloumi cheese
- 4 pork chops
- 1 tsp Greek seasoning

- Salt and pepper to taste
- ¼ cup all-purpose flour
- 2 tbsp bread crumbs

Directions:

1. Preheat air fryer to 190°C/380°F. Season the pork chops with Greek seasoning, salt and pepper. In a shallow bowl, add flour. In another shallow bowl, combine the crumbs and Halloumi. Dip the chops in the flour, then in the bread crumbs. Place them in the fryer and spray with cooking oil. Bake for 12-14 minutes, flipping once. Serve warm.

Variations & Ingredients Tips:

- Use feta cheese instead of Halloumi for a tangier flavor
- Add some dried herbs like oregano or thyme to the breading mixture
- Serve with a Greek salad and lemon potatoes

Per Serving: Calories: 277; Total Fat: 14g; Saturated Fat: 6g; Cholesterol: 80mg; Sodium: 417mg; Total Carbs: 10g; Dietary Fiber: 0g; Total Sugars: 0g; Protein: 28g

Korean-style Lamb Shoulder Chops

Servings: 3 | Prep Time: 15 Minutes | Cooking Time: 28 Minutes

Ingredients:

- ⅓ cup Regular or low-sodium soy sauce or gluten-free tamari sauce
- 1½ tablespoons Toasted sesame oil
- 1½ tablespoons Granulated white sugar
- 2 teaspoons Minced peeled fresh ginger
- 1 teaspoon Minced garlic
- ¼ teaspoon Red pepper flakes
- 3 170g bone-in lamb shoulder chops, any excess fat trimmed
- ⅔ cup Tapioca flour
- Vegetable oil spray

Directions:

1. Put the soy or tamari sauce, sesame oil, sugar, ginger, garlic, and red pepper flakes in a large, heavy zip-closed plastic bag. Add the chops, seal, and rub the marinade evenly over them through the bag. Refrigerate for at least 2 hours or up to 6 hours, turning the bag at least once so the chops move around in the marinade.
2. Set the bag out on the counter as the air fryer heats. Preheat the air fryer to 375°F/191°C.
3. Pour the tapioca flour on a dinner plate or in a small pie plate. Remove a chop from the marinade and dredge it on both sides in the tapioca flour, coating it evenly and well. Coat both sides with vegetable oil spray, set it in the basket, and dredge and spray the remaining chop(s), setting them in the basket in a single layer with space between them. Discard the bag with the marinade.
4. Air-fry, turning once, for 25 minutes, or until the chops are well browned and tender when pierced with the point of a paring knife. If the machine is at 360°F/182°C, you may need to add up to 3 minutes to the cooking time.
5. Use kitchen tongs to transfer the chops to a wire rack. Cool for just a couple of minutes before serving.

Variations & Ingredients Tips:

- Use lamb loin chops instead of shoulder for a leaner cut
- Add grated orange zest or juice to the marinade
- Serve with kimchi and steamed rice on the side

Per Serving: Calories: 410; Total Fat: 23g; Saturated Fat: 7g; Cholesterol: 90mg; Sodium: 1340mg; Total Carbs: 19g; Dietary Fiber: 1g; Total Sugars: 6g; Protein: 31g

Sirloin Steak Bites With Gravy

Servings: 4 | Prep Time: 10 Minutes | Cooking Time: 20 Minutes

Ingredients:

- 680 g sirloin steak, cubed
- 1 tablespoon olive oil
- 2 tablespoons cornstarch, divided
- 2 tablespoons soy sauce
- 2 tablespoons Worcestershire sauce
- 2 garlic cloves, minced
- Salt and pepper to taste
- ½ teaspoon smoked paprika
- ½ cup sliced red onion
- 2 fresh thyme sprigs
- ½ cup sliced mushrooms
- 1 cup beef broth
- 1 tablespoon butter

Directions:

1. Preheat air fryer to 200°C/400°F. Combine beef, olive oil, 1 tablespoon of cornstarch, garlic, pepper, Worcestershire sauce, soy sauce, thyme, salt, and paprika. Arrange the beef on the greased baking dish, then top with onions and mushrooms. Place the dish in the frying basket and bake for 4 minutes. While the beef is baking, whisk beef broth and the rest of the cornstarch in a small bowl. When the beef is ready, add butter and beef broth to the baking dish. Bake for another 5 minutes. Allow resting for 5 minutes. Serve and enjoy.

Variations & Ingredients Tips:

- Use chuck roast or stew meat instead of sirloin
- Add some baby potatoes or carrots to the dish
- Serve over mashed potatoes, egg noodles or rice

Per Serving: Calories: 382; Total Fat: 20g; Saturated Fat: 7g; Cholesterol: 122mg; Sodium: 809mg; Total Carbs: 8g; Dietary Fiber: 1g; Total Sugars: 2g; Protein: 41g

Perfect Pork Chops

Servings: 3 | Prep Time: 5 Minutes | Cooking Time: 10 Minutes

Ingredients:

- ¾ teaspoon mild paprika
- ¾ teaspoon dried thyme
- ¾ teaspoon onion powder
- ¼ teaspoon garlic powder
- ¼ teaspoon table salt
- ¼ teaspoon ground black pepper
- 3 boneless center-cut pork loin chops (170 g each)
- Vegetable oil spray

Directions:

1. Preheat the air fryer to 200°C/400°F.
2. Mix the paprika, thyme, onion powder, garlic powder, salt, and pepper in a small bowl until well combined. Massage this mixture into both sides of the chops. Generously coat both sides of the chops with vegetable oil spray.
3. When the machine is at temperature, set the chops in the basket with as much air space between them as possible. Air-fry undisturbed for 10 minutes, or until an instant-read meat thermometer inserted into the thickest part of a chop registers 65°C/145°F.
4. Use kitchen tongs to transfer the chops to a cutting board or serving plates. Cool for 5 minutes before serving.

Variations & Ingredients Tips:

- Use different types of seasoning, such as Cajun or Italian, for a variety of flavors.
- Add some minced garlic or red pepper flakes to the seasoning mixture for extra flavor.
- Serve the pork chops with a side of roasted vegetables or mashed potatoes for a complete meal.

Per Serving: Calories: 260; Total Fat: 13g; Saturated Fat: 4g; Cholesterol: 105mg; Sodium: 300mg; Total Carbs: 1g; Fiber: 0g; Sugars: 0g; Protein: 35g

Sloppy Joes

Servings: 4 | Prep Time: 10 Minutes | Cooking Time: 17 Minutes

Ingredients:

- oil for misting or cooking spray
- 454 g very lean ground beef
- 1 teaspoon onion powder
- ⅓ cup ketchup
- ¼ cup water
- ½ teaspoon celery seed
- 1 tablespoon lemon juice
- 1½ teaspoons brown sugar
- 1¼ teaspoons low-sodium Worcestershire sauce
- ½ teaspoon salt (optional)
- ½ teaspoon vinegar
- ⅛ teaspoon dry mustard
- hamburger or slider buns

Directions:

1. Spray air fryer basket with nonstick cooking spray or olive oil.
2. Break raw ground beef into small chunks and pile into basket.
3. Cook at 195°C/390°F for 5 minutes. Stir to break apart and cook 3 minutes. Stir and cook 4 minutes longer or until meat is well done.
4. Remove meat from air fryer, drain, and use a knife and fork to crumble into small pieces.
5. Give your air fryer basket a quick rinse to remove any bits of meat.
6. Place all the remaining ingredients except the buns in a 15 x 15 cm baking pan and mix together.
7. Add meat and stir well.

8. Cook at 165°C/330°F for 5 minutes. Stir and cook for 2 minutes.
9. Scoop onto buns.

Variations & Ingredients Tips:

- Use ground turkey or chicken for a lighter version
- Add diced bell peppers, carrots or zucchini to the meat mixture for extra veggies
- Top with sliced cheese, pickles or coleslaw for crunch and flavor

Per Serving: Calories: 325; Total Fat: 15g; Saturated Fat: 5g; Cholesterol: 81mg; Sodium: 632mg; Total Carbs: 19g; Dietary Fiber: 1g; Total Sugars: 9g; Protein: 28g

Balsamic Short Ribs

Servings: 2 | Prep Time: 10 Minutes + Marinating Time | Cooking Time: 30 Minutes

Ingredients:

- ⅛ tsp Worcestershire sauce
- ¼ cup olive oil
- ¼ cup balsamic vinegar
- ¼ cup chopped basil leaves
- ¼ cup chopped oregano
- 1 tbsp honey
- ¼ cup chopped fresh sage
- 3 cloves garlic, quartered
- ½ tsp salt
- 450 g beef short ribs

Directions:

1. Add all ingredients, except for the short ribs, to a plastic resealable bag and shake to combine. Reserve 2 tbsp of balsamic mixture in a small bowl. Place short ribs in the plastic bag and massage into ribs. Seal the bag and let marinate in the fridge for 30 minutes up to overnight. Preheat air fryer at 165°C/325°F. Place short ribs in the frying basket and bake for 16 minutes, turn once and brush with extra sauce. Serve warm.

Variations & Ingredients Tips:

- Use boneless beef chuck ribs or pork spare ribs instead of short ribs for a different cut of meat.
- Add a pinch of red pepper flakes or cayenne pepper to the marinade for a spicy kick.
- Serve over creamy polenta, mashed potatoes, or buttered noodles for a hearty meal.

Per Serving: Calories: 787; Total Fat: 71g; Saturated Fat: 22g; Cholesterol: 122mg; Sodium: 526mg; Total Carbs: 14g; Dietary Fiber: 1g; Total Sugars: 11g; Protein: 27g

Pork Schnitzel

Servings: 4 | Prep Time: 15 Minutes | Cooking Time: 14 Minutes

Ingredients:

- 4 boneless pork chops, pounded to 6 mm thickness
- 1 teaspoon salt, divided
- 1 teaspoon black pepper, divided
- ½ cup all-purpose flour
- 2 eggs
- 1 cup breadcrumbs
- ¼ teaspoon paprika
- 1 lemon, cut into wedges

Directions:

1. Season both sides of the pork chops with ½ teaspoon of the salt and ½ teaspoon of the pepper.
2. On a plate, place the flour.
3. In a large bowl, whisk the eggs.
4. In another large bowl, place the breadcrumbs.
5. Season the flour with the paprika and season the breadcrumbs with the remaining ½ teaspoon of salt and ½ teaspoon of pepper.
6. To bread the pork, place a pork chop in the flour, then into the whisked eggs, and then into the breadcrumbs. Place the breaded pork onto a plate and finish breading the remaining pork chops.
7. Preheat the air fryer to 200°C/390°F.
8. Place the pork chops into the air fryer, not overlapping and working in batches as needed. Spray the pork chops with cooking spray and cook for 8 minutes; flip the pork and cook for another 4 to 6 minutes or until cooked to an internal temperature of 63°C/145°F.
9. Serve with lemon wedges.

Variations & Ingredients Tips:

- Use chicken cutlets or thin slices of veal for variety
- Add some grated Parmesan cheese to the breadcrumbs for extra flavor
- Serve with German potato salad, sauerkraut or braised red cabbage

Per Serving: Calories: 368; Total Fat: 14g; Saturated Fat: 4g; Cholesterol: 167mg; Sodium: 813mg; Total Carbs:

27g; Dietary Fiber: 1g; Total Sugars: 2g; Protein: 34g

Honey Mesquite Pork Chops

Servings: 2 | Prep Time: 5 Minutes | Cooking Time: 10 Minutes

Ingredients:

- 2 tbsp mesquite seasoning
- ¼ cup honey
- 1 tbsp olive oil
- 1 tbsp water
- freshly ground black pepper
- 2 bone-in center cut pork chops (about 454 g)

Directions:

1. Whisk the mesquite seasoning, honey, olive oil, water and freshly ground black pepper together in a shallow glass dish. Pierce the chops all over and on both sides with a fork or meat tenderizer. Add the pork chops to the marinade and massage the marinade into the chops. Cover and marinate for 30 minutes.
2. Preheat the air fryer to 165°C/330°F.
3. Transfer the pork chops to the air fryer basket and pour half of the marinade over the chops, reserving the remaining marinade. Air-fry the pork chops for 6 minutes. Flip the pork chops over and pour the remaining marinade on top. Air-fry for an additional 3 minutes at 165°C/330°F. Then, increase the air fryer temperature to 200°C/400°F and air-fry the pork chops for an additional minute.
4. Transfer the pork chops to a serving plate, and let them rest for 5 minutes before serving. If you'd like a sauce for these chops, pour the cooked marinade from the bottom of the air fryer over the top.

Variations & Ingredients Tips:

- Try different spice rubs like cajun, jerk or five-spice powder
- Substitute the honey with maple syrup or brown sugar
- Serve with grilled pineapple or peach slices for a sweet-savory combo

Per Serving: Calories: 381; Total Fat: 18g; Saturated Fat: 4g; Cholesterol: 103mg; Sodium: 1148mg; Total Carbs: 25g; Dietary Fiber: 0g; Total Sugars: 24g; Protein: 31g

Santorini Steak Bowls

Servings: 2 | Prep Time: 15 Minutes | Cooking Time: 15 Minutes

Ingredients:

- 5 pitted Kalamata olives, halved
- 1 cucumber, diced
- 2 tomatoes, diced
- 1 tablespoon apple cider vinegar
- 2 teaspoons olive oil
- ¼ cup feta cheese crumbles
- ½ teaspoon Greek oregano
- ½ teaspoon dried dill
- ¼ teaspoon garlic powder
- ⅛ teaspoon ground nutmeg
- Salt and pepper to taste
- 1 (340 g) strip steak

Directions:

1. In a large bowl, combine cucumber, tomatoes, vinegar, olive oil, olives, and feta cheese. Let chill covered in the fridge until ready to use. Preheat air fryer to 200°C/400°F. Combine all spices in a bowl, then coat strip steak with this mixture. Add steak in the lightly greased frying basket and Air Fry for 10 minutes or until you reach your desired doneness, flipping once. Let sit onto a cutting board for 5 minutes. Thinly slice against the grain and divide between 2 bowls. Top with the cucumber mixture. Serve.

Variations & Ingredients Tips:

- Use chicken, lamb or shrimp instead of steak
- Add some chopped romaine lettuce or baby spinach
- Drizzle with tzatziki sauce or hummus for creamy texture

Per Serving: Calories: 449; Total Fat: 31g; Saturated Fat: 11g; Cholesterol: 106mg; Sodium: 559mg; Total Carbs: 10g; Dietary Fiber: 2g; Total Sugars: 5g; Protein: 34g

Pork Chops

Servings: 2 | Prep Time: 5 Minutes | Cooking Time: 16 Minutes

Ingredients:

- 2 bone-in, center-cut pork chops, 2.5 cm thick (280 g each)

- 2 teaspoons Worcestershire sauce
- Salt and pepper
- Cooking spray

Directions:

1. Rub the Worcestershire sauce into both sides of pork chops.
2. Season with salt and pepper to taste.
3. Spray air fryer basket with cooking spray and place the chops in basket side by side.
4. Cook at 180°C/360°F for 16 minutes or until well done. Let rest for 5 minutes before serving.

Variations & Ingredients Tips:

▶ Use different types of seasoning, such as garlic powder or smoked paprika, for a variety of flavors.
▶ Add some sliced onions or apples to the pork chops for extra flavor and texture.
▶ Serve the pork chops with a side of mashed potatoes or steamed vegetables for a classic comfort food meal.

Per Serving: Calories: 330; Total Fat: 17g; Saturated Fat: 6g; Cholesterol: 135mg; Sodium: 210mg; Total Carbs: 1g; Fiber: 0g; Sugars: 0g; Protein: 42g

Venison Backstrap

Servings: 4 | Prep Time: 15 Minutes | Cooking Time: 10 Minutes

Ingredients:

- 2 eggs
- 1/4 cup milk
- 1 cup whole wheat flour
- 1/2 teaspoon salt
- 1/4 teaspoon pepper
- 454g venison backstrap, sliced
- Salt and pepper
- Oil for misting or cooking spray

Directions:

1. Beat together eggs and milk in a shallow dish.
2. In another shallow dish, combine the flour, salt, and pepper. Stir to mix well.
3. Sprinkle venison steaks with additional salt and pepper to taste. Dip in flour, egg wash, then in flour again, pressing in coating.
4. Spray steaks with oil or cooking spray on both sides.
5. Cooking in 2 batches, place steaks in the air fryer basket in a single layer. Cook at 360°F/182°C for 8 minutes. Spray with oil, turn over, and spray other side. Cook for 2 minutes longer, until coating is crispy brown and meat is done to your liking.
6. Repeat to cook remaining venison.

Variations & Ingredients Tips:

▶ Use breadcrumbs or crushed pork rinds instead of flour for keto/low-carb
▶ Add cajun or blackening seasoning to the flour coating for a kick
▶ Serve with mushroom or pepper gravy on the side

Per Serving: Calories: 295; Total Fat: 9g; Saturated Fat: 3g; Cholesterol: 160mg; Sodium: 390mg; Total Carbs: 18g; Dietary Fiber: 2g; Total Sugars: 1g; Protein: 34g

Tuscan Veal Chops

Servings: 2 | Prep Time: 10 Minutes | Cooking Time: 12-15 Minutes

Ingredients:

- 4 teaspoons Olive oil
- 2 teaspoons Finely minced garlic
- 2 teaspoons Finely minced fresh rosemary leaves
- 1 teaspoon Finely grated lemon zest
- 1 teaspoon Crushed fennel seeds
- 1 teaspoon Table salt
- Up to 1/4 teaspoon Red pepper flakes
- 2 284g bone-in veal loin or rib chop(s), about 1.25cm thick

Directions:

1. Preheat the air fryer to 400°F/205°C.
2. Mix the oil, garlic, rosemary, lemon zest, fennel seeds, salt, and red pepper flakes in a small bowl. Rub this mixture onto both sides of the veal chop(s). Set aside at room temperature as the machine comes to temperature.
3. Set the chop(s) in the basket. If you're cooking more than one chop, leave as much air space between them as possible. Air-fry undisturbed for 12 minutes for medium-rare, or until an instant-read meat thermometer inserted into the center of a chop (without touching bone) registers 135°F/57°C (not USDA-approved). Or air-fry undisturbed for 15 minutes for medium-well, or until an instant-read meat thermometer registers 145°F/63°C (USDA-approved).

4. Use kitchen tongs to transfer the chops to a cutting board or a wire rack. Cool for 5 minutes before serving.

Variations & Ingredients Tips:

- Substitute dried herbs like oregano or thyme for the fresh rosemary
- Add grated parmesan to the herb coating for extra flavor
- Serve the chops with a lemon-caper sauce or red wine reduction

Per Serving: Calories: 370; Total Fat: 22g; Saturated Fat: 7g; Cholesterol: 190mg; Sodium: 730mg; Total Carbs: 2g; Dietary Fiber: 1g; Total Sugars: 0g; Protein: 39g

Cal-mex Chimichangas

Servings: 4 | Prep Time: 20 Minutes | Cooking Time: 30 Minutes

Ingredients:

- 1 can diced tomatoes with chiles
- 1 cup shredded cheddar
- 1/2 cup chopped onions
- 2 garlic cloves, minced
- 454g ground beef
- 2 tablespoons taco seasoning
- Salt and pepper to taste
- 4 flour tortillas
- 1/2 cup Pico de Gallo

Directions:

1. Warm the olive oil in a skillet over medium heat and stir-fry the onion and garlic for 3 minutes or until fragrant. Add ground beef, taco seasoning, salt and pepper. Stir and break up the beef with a spoon. Cook for 3-4 minutes or until it is browned. Stir in diced tomatoes with chiles. Scoop 1/2 cup of beef onto each tortilla. Form chimichangas by folding the sides of the tortilla into the middle, then roll up from the bottom. Use a toothpick to secure the chimichanga.
2. Preheat air fryer to 400°F/205°C. Lightly spray the chimichangas with cooking oil. Place the first batch in the fryer and Bake for 8 minutes. Transfer to a serving dish and top with shredded cheese and pico de gallo.

Variations & Ingredients Tips:

- Use ground turkey or chicken instead of beef for a leaner option
- Add drained black beans or corn to the filling
- Serve with sour cream, guacamole, and/or sliced avocado on the side

Per Serving: Calories: 659; Total Fat: 30g; Saturated Fat: 12g; Cholesterol: 132mg; Sodium: 1161mg; Total Carbs: 55g; Dietary Fiber: 6g; Total Sugars: 5g; Protein: 41g

Pork Schnitzel With Dill Sauce

Servings: 4 | Prep Time: 20 Minutes | Cooking Time: 4 Minutes

Ingredients:

- 6 boneless, center cut pork chops (about 680 g)
- ½ cup flour
- 1½ teaspoons salt
- freshly ground black pepper
- 2 eggs
- ½ cup milk
- 1½ cups toasted fine breadcrumbs
- 1 teaspoon paprika
- 3 tablespoons butter, melted
- 2 tablespoons vegetable or olive oil
- lemon wedges
- Dill Sauce:
- 1 cup chicken stock
- 1½ tablespoons cornstarch
- ⅓ cup sour cream
- 1½ tablespoons chopped fresh dill
- salt and pepper

Directions:

1. Trim the excess fat from the pork chops and pound each chop with a meat mallet between two pieces of plastic wrap until they are 3 cm thick.
2. Set up a dredging station. Combine the flour, salt, and black pepper in a shallow dish. Whisk the eggs and milk together in a second shallow dish. Finally, combine the breadcrumbs and paprika in a third shallow dish.
3. Dip each flattened pork chop in the flour. Shake off the excess flour and dip each chop into the egg mixture. Finally dip them into the breadcrumbs and press the breadcrumbs onto the meat firmly. Place each finished chop on a baking sheet until they are all coated.
4. Preheat the air fryer to 200°C/400°F.
5. Combine the melted butter and the oil in a small bowl and lightly brush both sides of the coated pork chops. Do not brush the chops too heavily or the breading will

not be as crispy.
6. Air-fry one schnitzel at a time for 4 minutes, turning it over halfway through the cooking time. Hold the cooked schnitzels warm on a baking pan in a 76°C/170°F oven while you finish air-frying the rest.
7. While the schnitzels are cooking, whisk the chicken stock and cornstarch together in a small saucepan over medium-high heat on the stovetop. Bring the mixture to a boil and simmer for 2 minutes. Remove the saucepan from heat and whisk in the sour cream. Add the chopped fresh dill and season with salt and pepper.
8. Transfer the pork schnitzel to a platter and serve with dill sauce and lemon wedges. For a traditional meal, serve this along side some egg noodles, spätzle or German potato salad.

Variations & Ingredients Tips:

- Use turkey cutlets or thin slices of eggplant for a change
- Add some Dijon mustard to the egg mixture for tangy flavor
- Garnish with capers, chopped parsley and sliced cucumbers

Per Serving: Calories: 662; Total Fat: 31g; Saturated Fat: 12g; Cholesterol: 238mg; Sodium: 1561mg; Total Carbs: 46g; Dietary Fiber: 2g; Total Sugars: 4g; Protein: 49g

Flank Steak With Roasted Peppers And Chimichurri

Servings: 4 | Prep Time: 30 Minutes | Cooking Time: 22 Minutes

Ingredients:

- 2 cups flat-leaf parsley leaves
- ¼ cup fresh oregano leaves
- 3 cloves garlic
- ½ cup olive oil
- ¼ cup red wine vinegar
- ½ tsp salt
- freshly ground black pepper
- ¼ tsp crushed red pepper flakes
- ½ tsp ground cumin
- 454 g flank steak
- 1 red bell pepper, cut into strips
- 1 yellow bell pepper, cut into strips

Directions:

1. Make the chimichurri sauce by chopping the parsley, oregano and garlic in a food processor. Add the olive oil, vinegar and seasonings and process again. Pour half of the sauce into a shallow dish with the flank steak and set the remaining sauce aside. Pierce the flank steak with a needle-style meat tenderizer or a paring knife and marinate the steak for 2 to 24 hours in the refrigerator. When you are ready to cook, remove the steak from the refrigerator and let it sit at room temperature for 30 minutes.
2. Preheat the air fryer to 200°C/400°F.
3. Cut the flank steak in half so that it fits more easily into the air fryer and transfer both pieces to the air fryer basket. Air-fry for 14 minutes, depending on how you like your steak cooked (10 minutes will give you medium for a 2.5 cm thick flank steak). Flip the steak over halfway through the cooking time.
4. When the flank steak is cooked to your liking, transfer it to a cutting board, loosely tent with foil and let it rest while you cook the peppers.
5. Toss the peppers in a little olive oil, salt and freshly ground black pepper and transfer them to the air fryer basket. Air-fry at 200°C/400°F for 8 minutes, shaking the basket once or twice throughout the cooking process. To serve, slice the flank steak against the grain of the meat and top with the roasted peppers. Drizzle the reserved chimichurri sauce on top, thinning the sauce with another 1 tbsp of olive oil if desired.

Variations & Ingredients Tips:

- Reserve some of the raw bell peppers to add color and crunch to the final dish
- Add some sliced red onions to the peppers for extra flavor
- Chimichurri is also great on chicken, pork or seafood

Per Serving: Calories: 540; Total Fat: 43g; Saturated Fat: 9g; Cholesterol: 68mg; Sodium: 529mg; Total Carbs: 6g; Dietary Fiber: 2g; Total Sugars: 2g; Protein: 31g

Asy Carnitas

Servings: 3 | Prep Time: 10 Minutes (plus Marinating Time) | Cooking Time: 25 Minutes

Ingredients:

- 680 g boneless country-style pork ribs, cut into 5 cm pieces
- ¼ cup orange juice
- 2 tablespoons brine from a jar of pickles, any type, even pickled jalapeño rings (gluten-free,

if a concern)
- 2 teaspoons minced garlic
- 2 teaspoons minced fresh oregano leaves
- ¾ teaspoon ground cumin
- ¾ teaspoon table salt
- ¾ teaspoon ground black pepper

Directions:

1. Mix the country-style pork rib pieces, orange juice, pickle brine, garlic, oregano, cumin, salt, and pepper in a large bowl. Cover and refrigerate for at least 2 hours or up to 10 hours, stirring the mixture occasionally.
2. Preheat the air fryer to 200°C/400°F. Set the rib pieces in their bowl on the counter as the machine heats.
3. Use kitchen tongs to transfer the rib pieces to the basket, arranging them in one layer. Some may touch. Air-fry for 25 minutes, turning and rearranging the pieces at the 10- and 20-minute marks to make sure all surfaces have been exposed to the air currents, until browned and sizzling.
4. Use clean kitchen tongs to transfer the rib pieces to a wire rack. Cool for a couple of minutes before serving.

Variations & Ingredients Tips:

- Use different types of citrus juice, such as lemon or lime, for a variety of flavors.
- Add some minced onion or jalapeño to the marinade for extra flavor.
- Serve the carnitas with warm tortillas, salsa, and guacamole for a classic Mexican meal.

Per Serving: Calories: 480; Total Fat: 30g; Saturated Fat: 10g; Cholesterol: 165mg; Sodium: 970mg; Total Carbs: 5g; Fiber: 0g; Sugars: 3g; Protein: 45g

Chicken-fried Steak

Servings: 2 | Prep Time: 15 Minutes | Cooking Time: 12 Minutes

Ingredients:

- 1½ cups all-purpose flour
- 2 large egg(s)
- 2 tablespoons regular or low-fat sour cream
- 2 tablespoons Worcestershire sauce
- 2 (115 g) thin beef cube steak(s)
- Vegetable oil spray

Directions:

1. Preheat the air fryer to 200°C/400°F.
2. Set up and fill two shallow soup plates or small pie plates on your counter: one for the flour; and one for the egg(s), whisked with the sour cream and Worcestershire sauce until uniform.
3. Dredge a piece of beef in the flour, coating it well on both sides and even along the edge. Shake off any excess; then dip the meat in the egg mixture, coating both sides while retaining the flour on the meat. Let any excess egg mixture slip back into the rest. Dredge the meat in the flour once again, coating all surfaces well. Gently shake off the excess coating and set the steak aside if you're coating another steak or two. Once done, coat the steak(s) on both sides with the vegetable oil spray.
4. Set the steak(s) in the basket. If there's more than one steak, make sure they do not overlap or even touch, although the smallest gap between them is enough to get them crunchy. Air-fry undisturbed for 6 minutes.
5. Use kitchen tongs to pick up one of the steaks. Coat it again on both sides with vegetable oil spray. Turn it upside down and set it back in the basket with that same regard for the space between them in larger batches. Repeat with any other steaks. Continue air-frying undisturbed for 6 minutes, or until golden brown and crunchy.
6. Use kitchen tongs to transfer the steak(s) to a wire rack. Cool for 5 minutes before serving.

Variations & Ingredients Tips:

- Use different types of steak, such as round or sirloin, for a variety of flavors and textures.
- Add some smoked paprika or cayenne pepper to the flour mixture for a spicy kick.
- Serve the chicken-fried steak with a side of gravy or creamy mashed potatoes for a classic comfort food meal.

Per Serving: Calories: 620; Total Fat: 24g; Saturated Fat: 9g; Cholesterol: 260mg; Sodium: 430mg; Total Carbs: 55g; Fiber: 2g; Sugars: 2g; Protein: 44g

German-style Pork Patties

Servings: 6 | Prep Time: 10 Minutes | Cooking Time: 35 Minutes

Ingredients:

- 450g ground pork
- ¼ cup diced fresh pear
- 1 tbsp minced sage leaves

- 1 garlic clove, minced
- 2 tbsp chopped chives
- Salt and pepper to taste

Directions:

1. Preheat the air fryer to 190°C/375°F. Combine the pork, pear, sage, chives, garlic, salt, and pepper in a bowl and mix gently but thoroughly with your hands, then make 8 patties about 3 cm thick. Lay the patties in the frying basket in a single layer and Air Fry for 15-20 minutes, flipping once halfway through. Remove and drain on paper towels, then serve. Serve and enjoy!

Variations & Ingredients Tips:

- Mix in some shredded apple for extra sweetness and moisture
- Serve on pretzel buns with grainy mustard and sauerkraut
- Form the patties around cubes of Swiss cheese for a melty surprise

Per Serving: Calories: 227; Total Fat: 17g; Saturated Fat: 6g; Cholesterol: 65mg; Sodium: 80mg; Total Carbs: 2g; Dietary Fiber: 0g; Total Sugars: 1g; Protein: 16g

Meat Loaves

Servings: 4 | Prep Time: 15 Minutes | Cooking Time: 19 Minutes

Ingredients:

- Sauce
- ¼ cup white vinegar
- ¼ cup brown sugar
- 2 tablespoons Worcestershire sauce
- ½ cup ketchup
- Meat Loaves
- 450 g very lean ground beef
- ⅔ cup dry bread (approx. 1 slice torn into small pieces)
- 1 egg
- ⅓ cup minced onion
- 1 teaspoon salt
- 2 tablespoons ketchup

Directions:

1. In a small saucepan, combine all sauce ingredients and bring to a boil. Remove from heat and stir to ensure that brown sugar dissolves completely.
2. In a large bowl, combine the beef, bread, egg, onion, salt, and ketchup. Mix well.
3. Divide meat mixture into 4 portions and shape each into a thick, round patty. Patties will be about 7.5 to 9 cm in diameter, and all four should fit easily into the air fryer basket at once.
4. Cook at 180°C/360°F for 18 minutes, until meat is well done. Baste tops of mini loaves with a small amount of sauce, and cook 1 minute.
5. Serve hot with additional sauce on the side.

Variations & Ingredients Tips:

- Use different types of ground meat, such as turkey or pork, for a variety of flavors.
- Add some grated carrot or zucchini to the meat mixture for extra moisture and nutrients.
- Serve the meat loaves with a side of mashed potatoes or green beans for a classic comfort food meal.

Per Serving: Calories: 330; Total Fat: 12g; Saturated Fat: 4.5g; Cholesterol: 115mg; Sodium: 1070mg; Total Carbs: 31g; Fiber: 1g; Sugars: 22g; Protein: 25g

Pork Chops With Cereal Crust

Servings: 2 | Prep Time: 10 Minutes | Cooking Time: 20 Minutes

Ingredients:

- ¼ cup grated Parmesan
- 1 egg
- 1 tablespoon Dijon mustard
- ¼ cup crushed bran cereal
- ¼ teaspoon black pepper
- ¼ teaspoon cumin powder
- ¼ teaspoon nutmeg
- 1 teaspoon horseradish powder
- 2 pork chops

Directions:

1. Preheat air fryer at 180°C/350°F. Whisk egg and mustard in a bowl. In another bowl, combine Parmesan cheese, cumin powder, nutmeg, horseradish powder, bran cereal, and black pepper.
2. Dip pork chops in the egg mixture, then dredge them in the cheese mixture.
3. Place pork chops in the frying basket and Air Fry for 12 minutes, tossing once.
4. Let rest onto a cutting board for 5 minutes. Serve.

Variations & Ingredients Tips:

- Use different types of cereal, such as cornflakes or panko breadcrumbs, for a variety of textures.
- Add some dried herbs, such as thyme or rosemary, to the cereal mixture for extra flavor.
- Serve the pork chops with a side of applesauce or sautéed spinach for a balanced meal.

Per Serving: Calories: 290; Total Fat: 14g; Saturated Fat: 6g; Cholesterol: 155mg; Sodium: 510mg; Total Carbs: 8g; Fiber: 2g; Sugars: 1g; Protein: 33g

Blossom Bbq Pork Chops

Servings: 2 | Prep Time: 10 Minutes | Cooking Time: 20 Minutes

Ingredients:

- 2 tbsp cherry preserves
- 1 tbsp honey
- 1 tbsp Dijon mustard
- 2 tsp light brown sugar
- 1 tsp Worcestershire sauce
- 1 tbsp lime juice
- 1 tbsp olive oil
- 2 cloves garlic, minced
- 1 tbsp chopped parsley
- 2 pork chops

Directions:

1. Mix all ingredients except pork chops in a bowl. Add pork chops and marinate covered in the fridge for 30 minutes.
2. Preheat air fryer to 177°C/350°F.
3. Place pork chops in the greased basket and air fry for 12 minutes at 177°C/350°F, turning once.
4. Let rest for 5 minutes before serving.

Variations & Ingredients Tips:

- Use bone-in or boneless pork chops
- Substitute orange juice for the lime juice
- Add 1 tsp smoked paprika or chipotle powder for a smoky flavor

Per Serving: Calories: 310; Total Fat: 12g; Saturated Fat: 3g; Cholesterol: 85mg; Sodium: 470mg; Total Carbs: 20g; Fiber: 1g; Sugars: 14g; Protein: 28g

Fish And Seafood Recipes

Shrimp Sliders With Avocado

Servings: 4 | Prep Time: 10 Minutes | Cooking Time: 10 Minutes

Ingredients:

- 16 raw jumbo shrimp, peeled, deveined, tails removed (about 450g)
- 1 rib celery, finely chopped
- 2 carrots, grated (about 1/2 cup)
- 2 teaspoons lemon juice
- 2 teaspoons Dijon mustard
- 1/4 cup chopped fresh basil or parsley
- 1/2 cup breadcrumbs
- 1/2 teaspoon salt
- Freshly ground black pepper
- Vegetable or olive oil, in a spray bottle
- 8 slider buns
- Mayonnaise
- Butter lettuce
- 2 avocados, sliced and peeled

Directions:

1. Pulse shrimp in a food processor until roughly chopped, reserving 1/4. Process remaining shrimp to a puree.
2. Combine all shrimp, celery, carrots, lemon, mustard, herbs, crumbs, salt and pepper.
3. Preheat air fryer to 190°C/380°F.
4. Form into 8 patties and spray both sides with oil.

5. Air-fry patties in batches for 10 minutes, flipping halfway.
6. Toast buns and spread with mayo. Build sliders with lettuce, patty and avocado.

Variations & Ingredients Tips:

- Use shrimp burgers on full size buns instead of sliders.
- Add cajun seasoning or hot sauce to the shrimp mixture.
- Top with remoulade sauce or slaw.

Per Serving: Calories: 320; Total Fat: 12g; Saturated Fat: 2g; Cholesterol: 170mg; Sodium: 760mg; Total Carbs: 30g; Dietary Fiber: 5g; Sugars: 3g; Protein: 22g

Herb-crusted Sole

Servings: 4 | Prep Time: 10 Minutes | Cooking Time: 20 Minutes

Ingredients:

- 1/2 lemon, juiced and zested
- 4 sole fillets
- 1/2 tsp dried thyme
- 1/2 tsp dried marjoram
- 1/2 tsp dried parsley
- Black pepper to taste
- 1 bread slice, crumbled
- 2 tsp olive oil

Directions:

1. Preheat air fryer to 160°C/320°F.
2. In a bowl, mix lemon zest, herbs, pepper, breadcrumbs and oil.
3. Arrange sole fillets skin-side down on a lined pan.
4. Pour lemon juice over fillets.
5. Press fillets into breadcrumb mixture to fully coat.
6. Air fry for 8-11 mins until breadcrumbs are crisp and golden.
7. Serve warm.

Variations & Ingredients Tips:

- Use tilapia, flounder or other thin white fish fillets.
- Add garlic powder, paprika or parmesan to the crumb mixture.
- Drizzle with melted butter or lemon butter before serving.

Per Serving: Calories: 147; Total Fat: 4g; Saturated Fat: 1g; Cholesterol: 60mg; Sodium: 193mg; Total Carbs: 8g; Dietary Fiber: 1g; Total Sugars: 1g; Protein: 19g

Tuna Nuggets In Hoisin Sauce

Servings: 4 | Prep Time: 10 Minutes | Cooking Time: 7 Minutes

Ingredients:

- 1/2 cup hoisin sauce
- 2 tablespoons rice wine vinegar
- 2 teaspoons sesame oil
- 1 teaspoon garlic powder
- 2 teaspoons dried lemongrass
- 1/4 teaspoon red pepper flakes
- 1/2 small onion, quartered and thinly sliced
- 225g fresh tuna, cut into 2.5-cm cubes
- Cooking spray
- 3 cups cooked jasmine rice

Directions:

1. Mix the hoisin sauce, vinegar, sesame oil, and seasonings together.
2. Stir in the onions and tuna nuggets.
3. Spray air fryer baking pan with nonstick spray and pour in tuna mixture.
4. Cook at 200°C/390°F for 3 minutes. Stir gently.
5. Cook 2 minutes and stir again, checking for doneness. Tuna should be barely cooked through, just beginning to flake and still very moist. If necessary, continue cooking and stirring in 1-minute intervals until done.
6. Serve warm over hot jasmine rice.

Variations & Ingredients Tips:

- Use salmon, swordfish or shrimp instead of tuna.
- Add some diced bell peppers or carrots to the mix.
- Serve over rice noodles or in lettuce wraps.

Per Serving: Calories: 350; Total Fat: 6g; Saturated Fat: 1g; Cholesterol: 30mg; Sodium: 950mg; Total Carbs: 54g; Dietary Fiber: 2g; Total Sugars: 13g; Protein: 22g

Fried Scallops

Servings: 3 | Prep Time: 10 Minutes | Cooking Time: 6 Minutes

Ingredients:

- 1/2 cup All-purpose flour or tapioca flour

- 1 Large egg, well beaten
- 2 cups Corn flake crumbs
- Up to 2 teaspoons Cayenne
- 1 teaspoon Celery seeds
- 1 teaspoon Table salt
- 450g Sea scallops
- Vegetable oil spray

Directions:

1. Preheat air fryer to 200°C/400°F.
2. Set up 3 dishes: one with flour, one with beaten egg, one with corn flake crumbs+cayenne+celery seeds+salt.
3. Dip scallops in flour, then egg, then corn flake mix to fully coat.
4. Generously spray scallops with oil on all sides.
5. Arrange scallops in air fryer basket with space between. Do not overcrowd.
6. Air fry for 6 minutes until lightly browned and firm.
7. Transfer to a wire rack and let cool 1-2 minutes before serving.

Variations & Ingredients Tips:

- Use panko breadcrumbs instead of corn flakes.
- Add Old Bay seasoning or lemon zest to the coating mix.
- Serve with lemon wedges or remoulade sauce.

Per Serving: Calories: 318; Total Fat: 2g; Saturated Fat: 1g; Cholesterol: 152mg; Sodium: 767mg; Total Carbs: 44g; Dietary Fiber: 1g; Total Sugars: 3g; Protein: 28g

Crabmeat-stuffed Flounder

Servings: 3 | Prep Time: 20 Minutes | Cooking Time: 12 Minutes

Ingredients:

- 130g purchased backfin or claw crabmeat, picked over for bits of shell and cartilage
- 6 saltine crackers, crushed into fine crumbs
- 2 tablespoons plus 1 teaspoon regular or low-fat mayonnaise (not fat-free)
- 3/4 teaspoon yellow prepared mustard
- 1 1/2 teaspoons Worcestershire sauce
- 1/8 teaspoon celery salt
- 3 (140-170g) skinless flounder fillets
- Vegetable oil spray
- Mild paprika

Directions:

1. Preheat the air fryer to 200°C/400°F.
2. Gently mix the crabmeat, crushed saltines, mayonnaise, mustard, Worcestershire sauce, and celery salt in a bowl until well combined.
3. Generously coat the flat side of a fillet with vegetable oil spray. Set the fillet sprayed side down on your work surface. Cut the fillet in half widthwise, then cut one of the halves in half lengthwise. Set a scant 1/3 cup of the crabmeat mixture on top of the undivided half of the fish fillet, mounding the mixture to make an oval that somewhat fits the shape of the fillet with at least a 6-mm border of fillet beyond the filling all around.
4. Take the two thin divided quarters (that is, the halves of the half) and lay them lengthwise over the filling, overlapping at each end and leaving a little space in the middle where the filling peeks through. Coat the top of the stuffed flounder piece with vegetable oil spray, then sprinkle paprika over the stuffed flounder fillet. Set aside and use the remaining fillet(s) to make more stuffed flounder "packets," repeating steps 3 and
5. Use a nonstick-safe spatula to transfer the stuffed flounder fillets to the basket. Leave as much space between them as possible. Air-fry undisturbed for 12 minutes, or until lightly brown and firm (but not hard).
6. Use that same spatula, plus perhaps another one, to transfer the fillets to a serving platter or plates. Cool for a minute or two, then serve hot.

Variations & Ingredients Tips:

- Stuff with shrimp or lobster meat instead of crab.
- Sprinkle with Old Bay seasoning in addition to the paprika.
- Serve with a lemon beurre blanc or hollandaise sauce.

Per Serving: Calories: 250; Total Fat: 10g; Saturated Fat: 1.5g; Cholesterol: 140mg; Sodium: 660mg; Total Carbs: 9g; Dietary Fiber: 0g; Total Sugars: 1g; Protein: 31g

Crispy Fish Sandwiches

Servings: 4 | Prep Time: 15 Minutes | Cooking Time: 25 Minutes

Ingredients:

- 1/2 cup torn iceberg lettuce
- 1/2 cup mayonnaise
- 1 tbsp Dijon mustard
- 1/2 cup diced dill pickles

- 1 tsp capers
- 1 tsp tarragon
- 1 tsp dill
- Salt and pepper to taste
- 1/3 cup flour
- 2 tbsp cornstarch
- 1 tsp smoked paprika
- 1/4 cup milk
- 1 egg
- 1/2 cup bread crumbs
- 4 cod fillets, cut in half
- 1 vine-ripe tomato, sliced
- 4 hamburger buns

Directions:

1. Mix the mayonnaise, mustard, pickles, capers, tarragon, dill, salt, and pepper in a small bowl and let the resulting tartare sauce chill covered in the fridge until ready to use.
2. Preheat air fryer at 190°C/375°F. In a bowl, mix the flour, cornstarch, paprika, and salt. In another bowl, beat the milk and egg and in a third bowl, add the breadcrumbs.
3. Roll the cod in the flour mixture, shake off excess flour. Then, dip in the egg, shake off excess egg. Finally, dredge in the breadcrumbs mixture.
4. Place fish pieces in the greased frying basket and Air Fry for 6 minutes, flipping once.
5. Add cooked fish, lettuce, tomato slices, and tartar sauce to each bottom bun and top with the top bun. Serve.

Variations & Ingredients Tips:

- Use haddock, pollack or catfish instead of cod.
- Add some hot sauce or cayenne to the tartar sauce for a spicy kick.
- Toast the buns before assembling for extra crunch.

Per Serving: Calories: 530; Total Fat: 28g; Saturated Fat: 5g; Cholesterol: 115mg; Sodium: 1050mg; Total Carbs: 46g; Dietary Fiber: 2g; Total Sugars: 8g; Protein: 29g

Mediterranean Sea Scallops

Servings: 2 | Prep Time: 15 Minutes | Cooking Time: 20 Minutes

Ingredients:

- 1 tbsp olive oil
- 1 shallot, minced
- 2 tbsp capers
- 2 cloves garlic, minced
- 1/2 cup heavy cream
- 3 tbsp butter
- 1 tbsp lemon juice
- Salt and pepper to taste
- 1/4 tbsp cumin powder
- 1/4 tbsp curry powder
- 450g jumbo sea scallops
- 2 tbsp chopped parsley
- 1 tbsp chopped cilantro

Directions:

1. Warm the olive oil in a saucepan over medium heat. Add shallot and stir-fry for 2 minutes until translucent.
2. Stir in capers, cumin, curry, garlic, heavy cream, 1 tbsp butter, lemon juice, salt and pepper and cook for 2 minutes until boiling. Lower heat and simmer 3 minutes until sauce thickens. Turn off heat.
3. Preheat air fryer at 200°C/400°F.
4. In a bowl, add remaining 2 tbsp butter and scallops and toss to coat all sides.
5. Place scallops in greased frying basket and Air Fry for 8 minutes, flipping once.
6. Drizzle caper sauce over, scatter with parsley, cilantro and serve.

Variations & Ingredients Tips:

- Use bay scallops instead of jumbo.
- Add white wine or vegetable broth to the sauce.
- Serve over linguine or zucchini noodles.

Per Serving: Calories: 430, Total Fat: 32g, Saturated Fat: 16g, Cholesterol: 135mg, Sodium: 590mg, Total Carbs: 10g, Fiber: 1g, Sugars: 2g, Protein: 28g

Malaysian Shrimp With Sambal Mayo

Servings: 4 | Prep Time: 15 Minutes | Cooking Time: 30 Minutes

Ingredients:

- 24 jumbo shrimp, peeled and deveined
- 2/3 cup panko breadcrumbs
- 3 tbsp mayonnaise
- 1 tbsp sambal oelek paste
- 2/3 cup shredded coconut
- 1 lime, zested
- 1/2 tsp ground coriander
- Salt to taste

- 2 tbsp flour
- 2 eggs

Directions:

1. Make sambal mayo by mixing mayonnaise and sambal oelek paste. Set aside.
2. In a bowl, mix coconut, lime zest, coriander, panko and salt.
3. Place flour in one shallow bowl and whisked eggs in another.
4. Season shrimp with salt. Dredge in flour, dip in egg, then coat in coconut mixture, pressing gently to adhere.
5. Preheat air fryer to 180°C/360°F.
6. Arrange shrimp in a single layer in greased air fryer basket.
7. Air fry for 8 minutes, flipping once, until golden and cooked through.
8. Serve hot shrimp with sambal mayo for dipping.

Variations & Ingredients Tips:

- Use sweetened shredded coconut for a sweeter crust.
- Add curry powder or red pepper flakes to the coconut mixture.
- Serve shrimp over a salad or with rice on the side.

Per Serving (6 shrimp): Calories: 249; Total Fat: 13g; Saturated Fat: 6g; Cholesterol: 173mg; Sodium: 464mg; Total Carbs: 20g; Dietary Fiber: 2g; Total Sugars: 2g; Protein: 15g

Oyster Shrimp With Fried Rice

Servings: 4 | Prep Time: 20 Minutes | Cooking Time: 40 Minutes

Ingredients:

- 450g peeled shrimp, deveined
- 1 shallot, chopped
- 2 garlic cloves, minced
- 1 tbsp olive oil
- 1 tbsp butter
- 2 eggs, beaten
- 2 cups cooked rice
- 1 cup baby peas
- 2 tbsp fish sauce
- 1 tbsp oyster sauce

Directions:

1. Preheat the air fryer to 190°C/370°F.
2. Combine the shrimp, shallot, garlic, and olive oil in a cake pan. Put the cake pan in the air fryer and Bake the shrimp for 5-7 minutes, stirring once until shrimp are no longer opaque.
3. Remove into a bowl, and set aside. Put the butter in the hot cake pan to melt. Add the eggs and return to the fryer. Bake for 4-6 minutes, stirring once until the eggs are set. Remove the eggs from the pan and set aside.
4. Add the rice, peas, oyster sauce, and fish sauce to the pan and return it to the fryer. Bake for 12-15 minutes, stirring once halfway through.
5. Pour in the shrimp and eggs and stir. Cook for 2-3 more minutes until everything is hot.

Variations & Ingredients Tips:

- Add diced carrots, peas or other veggies to the fried rice.
- Use cooked chicken or beef instead of shrimp.
- Drizzle with soy sauce or sriracha before serving.

Per Serving: Calories: 320; Total Fat: 9g; Saturated Fat: 3g; Cholesterol: 280mg; Sodium: 1120mg; Total Carbs: 35g; Dietary Fiber: 2g; Sugars: 2g; Protein: 27g

Shrimp, Chorizo And Fingerling Potatoes

Servings: 4 | Prep Time: 10 Minutes | Cooking Time: 16 Minutes

Ingredients:

- 1/2 red onion, chopped into 2.5cm chunks
- 8 fingerling potatoes, sliced into 2.5cm slices or halved lengthwise
- 1 teaspoon olive oil
- Salt and freshly ground black pepper
- 225g raw chorizo sausage, sliced into 2.5cm chunks
- 16 raw large shrimp, peeled, deveined and tails removed
- 1 lime
- 1/4 cup chopped fresh cilantro
- Chopped orange zest (optional)

Directions:

1. Preheat air fryer to 190°C/380°F.
2. Toss onion and potato chunks with olive oil, salt and pepper in a bowl.
3. Transfer veggies to air fryer basket and air-fry for 6

minutes, shaking basket periodically.
4. Add chorizo chunks and air-fry for 5 more minutes.
5. Add shrimp, season with salt and air-fry for 5 more minutes, shaking occasionally.
6. Transfer contents to a bowl and squeeze lime juice over top. Toss with cilantro, orange zest and drizzle of olive oil. Season to taste.
7. Serve with a green salad.

Variations & Ingredients Tips:

- Use cooked shrimp or a different sausage like chicken or turkey.
- Add smoked paprika or crushed red pepper for extra flavor.
- Serve in tortillas or over rice instead of a salad.

Per Serving: Calories: 400; Total Fat: 20g; Saturated Fat: 6g; Cholesterol: 170mg; Sodium: 760mg; Total Carbs: 29g; Dietary Fiber: 3g; Sugars: 2g; Protein: 26g

Summer Sea Scallops

Servings: 4 | Prep Time: 10 Minutes | Cooking Time: 30 Minutes

Ingredients:

- 1 cup asparagus
- 1 cup peas
- 1 cup chopped broccoli
- 2 tsp olive oil
- ½ tsp dried oregano
- 340g sea scallops

Directions:

1. Preheat air fryer to 200°C/400°F.
2. Add the asparagus, peas, and broccoli to a bowl and mix with olive oil.
3. Put the bowl in the fryer and Air Fry for 4-6 minutes until crispy and soft. Take the veggies out and add the herbs; let sit.
4. Add the scallops to the fryer and Air Fry for 4-5 minutes until the scallops are springy to the touch.
5. Serve immediately with the vegetables. Enjoy!

Variations & Ingredients Tips:

- Use green beans, zucchini or cherry tomatoes instead of broccoli.
- Toss the vegetables with lemon juice and garlic for extra flavor.
- Serve over a bed of quinoa, couscous or pasta.

Per Serving: Calories: 180; Total Fat: 4g; Saturated Fat: 0.5g; Cholesterol: 50mg; Sodium: 880mg; Total Carbs: 12g; Dietary Fiber: 3g; Total Sugars: 4g; Protein: 24g

The Best Oysters Rockefeller

Servings: 2 | Prep Time: 20 Minutes | Cooking Time: 30 Minutes

Ingredients:

- 4 tsp grated Parmesan
- 2 tbsp butter
- 1 sweet onion, minced
- 1 clove garlic, minced
- 1 cup baby spinach
- 1/8 tsp Tabasco hot sauce
- 1/2 tsp lemon juice
- 1/2 tsp lemon zest
- 1/4 cup bread crumbs
- 12 oysters, on the half shell

Directions:

1. Melt butter in a skillet over medium heat. Stir in onion, garlic, and spinach and stir-fry for 3 minutes until the onion is translucent. Mix in Parmesan cheese, hot sauce, lemon juice, lemon zest, and bread crumbs. Divide this mixture between the tops of oysters.
2. Preheat air fryer to 200°C/400°F. Place oysters in the frying basket and Air Fry for 6 minutes.
3. Serve immediately.

Variations & Ingredients Tips:

- Substitute spinach with kale, arugula or watercress.
- Add some crispy bacon bits or pancetta to the topping.
- Serve with lemon wedges and hot sauce on the side.

Per Serving: Calories: 370; Total Fat: 25g; Saturated Fat: 13g; Cholesterol: 125mg; Sodium: 510mg; Total Carbs: 21g; Dietary Fiber: 2g; Total Sugars: 4g; Protein: 17g

Crab Cakes On A Budget

Servings: 4 | Prep Time: 15 Minutes | Cooking Time: 12 Minutes

Ingredients:

- 225g imitation crabmeat
- 115g leftover cooked fish (such as cod, pol-

- lock, or haddock)
- 2 tablespoons minced green onion
- 2 tablespoons minced celery
- 3/4 cup crushed saltine cracker crumbs
- 2 tablespoons light mayonnaise
- 1 teaspoon prepared yellow mustard
- 1 tablespoon Worcestershire sauce, plus 2 teaspoons
- 2 teaspoons dried parsley flakes
- 1/2 teaspoon dried dill weed, crushed
- 1/2 teaspoon garlic powder
- 1/2 teaspoon Old Bay Seasoning
- 1/2 cup panko breadcrumbs
- Oil for misting or cooking spray

Directions:

1. Use knives or a food processor to finely shred crabmeat and fish.
2. In a large bowl, combine all ingredients except panko and oil. Stir well.
3. Shape into 8 small, fat patties.
4. Carefully roll patties in panko crumbs to coat. Spray both sides with oil or cooking spray.
5. Place patties in air fryer basket and cook at 200°C/390°F for 12 minutes or until golden brown and crispy.

Variations & Ingredients Tips:

- Use canned salmon or tuna instead of imitation crab.
- Add some minced red bell pepper or jalapeño for color and heat.
- Serve with a spicy remoulade or Sriracha mayo dipping sauce.

Per Serving: Calories: 240; Total Fat: 8g; Saturated Fat: 1.5g; Cholesterol: 75mg; Sodium: 820mg; Total Carbs: 23g; Dietary Fiber: 1g; Total Sugars: 2g; Protein: 18g

Cheese & Crab Stuffed Mushrooms

Servings: 2 | Prep Time: 20 Minutes | Cooking Time: 30 Minutes

Ingredients:

- 170 grams lump crabmeat, shells discarded
- 170 grams mascarpone cheese, softened
- 2 jalapeño peppers, minced
- ¼ cup diced red onions
- 2 tsp grated Parmesan cheese
- 2 portobello mushroom caps
- 2 tbsp butter, divided
- ½ tsp prepared horseradish
- ¼ tsp Worcestershire sauce
- ¼ tsp smoked paprika
- Salt and pepper to taste
- ¼ cup bread crumbs

Directions:

1. Melt 1 tbsp of butter in a skillet over heat for 30 seconds. Add in onion and cook for 3 minutes until tender. Stir in mascarpone cheese, Parmesan cheese, horseradish, jalapeño peppers, Worcestershire sauce, paprika, salt and pepper and cook for 2 minutes until smooth. Fold in crabmeat. Spoon mixture into mushroom caps. Set aside.
2. Preheat air fryer at 180°C/350°F.
3. Microwave the remaining butter until melted. Stir in breadcrumbs. Scatter over stuffed mushrooms.
4. Place mushrooms in the greased air fryer basket and Bake for 8 minutes.
5. Serve immediately.

Variations & Ingredients Tips:

- Substitute crab with cooked shrimp, lobster, or scallops.
- Use button mushrooms, cremini, or shiitake caps instead of portobellos.
- Top with shredded cheddar, Gruyère, or Monterey Jack cheese before baking.

Per Serving: Calories: 520; Total Fat: 44g; Saturated Fat: 25g; Sodium: 860mg; Total Carbohydrates: 13g; Dietary Fiber: 2g; Total Sugars: 4g; Protein: 22g

Kid's Flounder Fingers

Servings: 4 | Prep Time: 10 Minutes | Cooking Time: 45 Minutes

Ingredients:

- 450g catfish flounder fillets, cut into 2.5cm chunks
- 1/2 cup seasoned fish fry breading mix

Directions:

1. Preheat air fryer to 200°C/400°F.
2. In a resealable bag, add flounder chunks and breading mix.
3. Seal and shake bag until fish is coated.

4. Place coated nuggets in a single layer in greased air fryer basket.
5. Air fry for 18-20 minutes, shaking basket once, until crisp.
6. Serve warm.

Variations & Ingredients Tips:

- Use any firm white fish like cod or haddock.
- Make your own seasoned breadcrumb mix with spices.
- Serve with tartar sauce, ketchup or ranch for dipping.

Per Serving: Calories: 167; Total Fat: 2g; Saturated Fat: 0g; Cholesterol: 51mg; Sodium: 513mg; Total Carbs: 13g; Dietary Fiber: 0g; Total Sugars: 1g; Protein: 23g

Black Cod With Grapes, Fennel, Pecans And Kale

Servings: 2 | Prep Time: 10 Minutes | Cooking Time: 15 Minutes

Ingredients:

- 2 (170-225g) fillets of black cod (or sablefish)
- Salt and freshly ground black pepper
- Olive oil
- 1 cup grapes, halved
- 1 small bulb fennel, sliced 6-mm thick
- ½ cup pecans
- 3 cups shredded kale
- 2 teaspoons white balsamic vinegar or white wine vinegar
- 2 tablespoons extra virgin olive oil

Directions:

1. Preheat the air fryer to 200°C/400°F.
2. Season the cod fillets with salt and pepper and drizzle, brush or spray a little olive oil on top. Place the fish, presentation side up (skin side down), into the air fryer basket. Air-fry for 10 minutes.
3. When the fish has finished cooking, remove the fillets to a side plate and loosely tent with foil to rest.
4. Toss the grapes, fennel and pecans in a bowl with a drizzle of olive oil and season with salt and pepper. Add the grapes, fennel and pecans to the air fryer basket and air-fry for 5 minutes at 200°C/400°F, shaking the basket once during the cooking time.
5. Transfer the grapes, fennel and pecans to a bowl with the kale. Dress the kale with the balsamic vinegar and olive oil, season to taste with salt and pepper and serve along side the cooked fish.

Variations & Ingredients Tips:

- Use salmon, halibut or sea bass instead of black cod.
- Substitute grapes with sliced apples or pears.
- Toast the pecans before air frying for extra nuttiness.

Per Serving: Calories: 540; Total Fat: 35g; Saturated Fat: 5g; Cholesterol: 100mg; Sodium: 370mg; Total Carbs: 24g; Dietary Fiber: 6g; Total Sugars: 14g; Protein: 38g

Panko-breaded Cod Fillets

Servings: 2 | Prep Time: 10 Minutes | Cooking Time: 20 Minutes

Ingredients:

- 1 lemon wedge, juiced and zested
- 1/2 cup panko bread crumbs
- Salt to taste
- 1 tbsp Dijon mustard
- 1 tbsp butter, melted
- 2 cod fillets

Directions:

1. Preheat air fryer to 175°C/350°F.
2. Combine all ingredients, except for the fish, in a bowl.
3. Press mixture evenly across tops of cod fillets.
4. Place fillets in the greased frying basket and Air Fry for 10 minutes until the cod is opaque and flakes easily with a fork.
5. Serve immediately.

Variations & Ingredients Tips:

- Use other white fish like haddock or pollock.
- Add grated parmesan or breadcrumbs to the panko coating.
- Serve with lemon wedges and tartar sauce.

Per Serving: Calories: 240; Total Fat: 7g; Saturated Fat: 3g; Cholesterol: 70mg; Sodium: 460mg; Total Carbs: 14g; Dietary Fiber: 1g; Sugars: 1g; Protein: 28g

Sweet Potato-wrapped Shrimp

Servings: 3 | Prep Time: 15 Minutes | Cooking Time: 6 Minutes

Ingredients:

- 24 Long spiralized sweet potato strands
- Olive oil spray
- ¼ tsp garlic powder
- ¼ tsp table salt
- Up to a ⅛ tsp cayenne
- 12 Large shrimp (20–25 per g), peeled and deveined

Directions:

1. Preheat the air fryer to 200°C/400°F.
2. Lay the spiralized sweet potato strands on a large swath of paper towels and straighten out the strands to long ropes. Coat them with olive oil spray, then sprinkle them with the garlic powder, salt, and cayenne.
3. Pick up 2 strands and wrap them around the center of a shrimp, with the ends tucked under what now becomes the bottom side of the shrimp. Continue wrapping the remainder of the shrimp.
4. Set the shrimp bottom side down in the basket with as much air space between them as possible. Air-fry undisturbed for 6 minutes, or until the sweet potato strands are crisp and the shrimp are pink and firm.
5. Use kitchen tongs to transfer the shrimp to a wire rack. Cool for only a minute or two before serving.

Variations & Ingredients Tips:

- Use zucchini noodles instead of sweet potato for a different flavor and texture.
- Add some paprika or chili powder to the seasoning mix for extra heat.
- Serve with a dipping sauce like sweet chili or garlic aioli.

Per Serving: Calories: 120; Total Fat: 1g; Saturated Fat: 0g; Cholesterol: 110mg; Sodium: 420mg; Total Carbohydrates: 12g; Dietary Fiber: 2g; Total Sugars: 3g; Protein: 14g

Corn & Shrimp Boil

Servings: 4 | Prep Time: 15 Minutes | Cooking Time: 40 Minutes

Ingredients:

- 8 frozen "mini" corn on the cob
- 1 tbsp smoked paprika
- 2 tsp dried thyme
- 1 tsp dried marjoram
- 1 tsp sea salt
- 1 tsp garlic powder
- 1 tsp onion powder
- 1 tsp cayenne pepper
- 450g baby potatoes, halved
- 1 tbsp olive oil
- 450g peeled shrimp, deveined
- 1 avocado, sliced

Directions:

1. Preheat the air fryer to 190°C/370°F.
2. Combine the paprika, thyme, marjoram, salt, garlic, onion, and cayenne and mix well. Pour into a small glass jar.
3. Add the potatoes, corn, and olive oil to the frying basket and sprinkle with 2 tsp of the spice mix and toss. Air Fry for 15 minutes, shaking the basket once until tender. Remove and set aside.
4. Put the shrimp in the frying basket and sprinkle with 2 tsp of the spice mix. Air Fry for 5-8 minutes, shaking once until shrimp are tender and pink.
5. Combine all the ingredients in the frying basket and sprinkle with 2 tsp of the spice mix. Toss to coat and cook for 1-2 more minutes or until hot.
6. Serve topped with avocado.

Variations & Ingredients Tips:

- Add some sliced andouille sausage or bacon to the mix.
- Squeeze some lemon juice over the top before serving.
- Sprinkle with chopped fresh parsley or dill.

Per Serving: Calories: 380; Total Fat: 16g; Saturated Fat: 2.5g; Cholesterol: 180mg; Sodium: 1220mg; Total Carbs: 40g; Dietary Fiber: 8g; Total Sugars: 5g; Protein: 27g

Asian-style Salmon Fillets

Servings: 4 | Prep Time: 15 Minutes | Cooking Time: 15 Minutes

Ingredients:

- 1 tbsp sesame oil
- 2 tbsp miso paste
- 2 tbsp tamari
- 2 tbsp soy sauce
- 2 tbsp dark brown sugar
- 1/2 tsp garlic powder
- 1/2 tsp ginger powder
- 4 salmon fillets

- 4 cups cooked brown rice
- 4 lemon slices

Directions:

1. Preheat air fryer at 190°C/375°F. In a bowl, combine all ingredients, except for salmon and cooked rice.
2. Add 1/3 of the marinade to a shallow dish, submerge salmon fillets and let marinate covered in the fridge for 10 minutes. Reserve the remaining marinade.
3. Place salmon fillets, skin side up, in the greased frying basket and Air Fry for 6-8 minutes, turning once, and brush with the reserved marinade.
4. Divide cooked rice into serving dishes and top each with a salmon fillet. Pour the remaining marinade on top and serve with lemon slices on the side.

Variations & Ingredients Tips:

▶ Use honey or maple syrup instead of brown sugar.
▶ Add a sprinkle of toasted sesame seeds before serving.
▶ Serve with stir-fried veggies or soba noodles.

Per Serving: Calories: 510; Total Fat: 22g; Saturated Fat: 4g; Cholesterol: 95mg; Sodium: 1180mg; Total Carbs: 46g; Dietary Fiber: 3g; Total Sugars: 10g; Protein: 36g

Breaded Parmesan Perch

Servings: 5 | Prep Time: 10 Minutes | Cooking Time: 15 Minutes

Ingredients:

- 1/4 cup grated Parmesan
- 1/2 tsp salt
- 1/4 tsp paprika
- 1 tbsp chopped dill
- 1 tsp dried thyme
- 2 tsp Dijon mustard
- 2 tbsp bread crumbs
- 4 ocean perch fillets
- 1 lemon, quartered
- 2 tbsp chopped cilantro

Directions:

1. Preheat air fryer to 200°C/400°F.
2. Combine salt, paprika, pepper, dill, mustard, thyme, Parmesan, and bread crumbs in a wide bowl.
3. Coat all sides of the fillets in the breading, then transfer to the greased frying basket.
4. Air Fry for 8 minutes until outside is golden and the inside is cooked through.
5. Garnish with lemon wedges and sprinkle with cilantro. Serve and enjoy!

Variations & Ingredients Tips:

▶ Use cod, haddock or flounder instead of perch.
▶ Add some lemon zest or garlic powder to the breading.
▶ Serve with a side of tartar sauce or marinara sauce.

Per Serving: Calories: 120; Total Fat: 4.5g; Saturated Fat: 1.5g; Cholesterol: 55mg; Sodium: 430mg; Total Carbs: 3g; Dietary Fiber: 0g; Total Sugars: 0g; Protein: 17g

Vegetarian Recipes

Mexican Twice Air-fried Sweet Potatoes

Servings: 2 | Prep Time: 15 Minutes | Cooking Time: 42 Minutes

Ingredients:

- 2 large sweet potatoes
- Olive oil
- Salt and freshly ground black pepper
- 1/3 cup diced red onion
- 1/3 cup diced red bell pepper
- 1/2 cup canned black beans, drained and rinsed

- 1/2 cup corn kernels, fresh or frozen
- 1/2 teaspoon chili powder
- 1 1/2 cups grated pepper jack cheese, divided
- Jalapeño peppers, sliced

Directions:

1. Preheat the air fryer to 200°C/400°F.
2. Rub the sweet potatoes with olive oil and season with salt and pepper. Air fry at 400°F for 30 minutes, rotating occasionally.
3. Make the filling: Sauté onion and pepper. Add black beans, corn, and chili powder and sauté for 3 minutes. Set aside.
4. Remove potatoes, let rest 5 minutes. Slice off one cm of the flattest sides.
5. Scoop out potato flesh into a bowl, leaving 1.3-cm around edges.
6. Mash potato flesh. Add filling and 1 cup cheese. Season and mix well.
7. Stuff potato shells with filling, mounding high.
8. Air fry stuffed potatoes at 190°C/370°F for 10 minutes.
9. Top with remaining cheese, lower heat to 170°C/340°F and cook 2 more minutes to melt cheese.
10. Top with jalapeños and serve warm.

Variations & Ingredients Tips:

- Use vegan cheese shreds for a dairy-free option.
- Add diced avocado or pico de gallo as toppers.
- Swap black beans for pinto or kidney beans.

Per Serving: Calories: 653; Total Fat: 27g; Saturated Fat: 14g; Sodium: 877mg; Total Carbohydrates: 82g; Dietary Fiber: 16g; Total Sugars: 15g; Protein: 25g

Garlicky Roasted Mushrooms

Servings: 4 | Prep Time: 10 Minutes | Cooking Time: 30 Minutes

Ingredients:

- 16 garlic cloves, peeled
- 2 tsp olive oil
- 16 button mushrooms
- 2 tbsp fresh chives, snipped
- Salt and pepper to taste
- 1 tbsp white wine

Directions:

1. Preheat air fryer to 175°C/350°F. Coat the garlic with some olive oil in a baking pan, then Roast in the air fryer for 12 minutes. When done, take the pan out and stir in the mushrooms, salt, and pepper. Then add the remaining olive oil and white wine. Put the pan back into the fryer and Bake for 10-15 minutes until the mushrooms and garlic soften. Sprinkle with chives and serve warm.

Variations & Ingredients Tips:

- Use a variety of mushrooms like cremini, portobello or oyster for different flavors.
- Add a splash of balsamic vinegar or lemon juice before serving.
- Toss in fresh herbs like thyme or rosemary.

Per Serving: Calories: 90; Total Fat: 4g; Saturated Fat: 0.5g; Sodium: 10mg; Total Carbs: 12g; Dietary Fiber: 2g; Total Sugars: 1g; Protein: 3g

Charred Cauliflower Tacos

Servings: 4 | Prep Time: 15 Minutes | Cooking Time: 10 Minutes

Ingredients:

- 1 head cauliflower, washed and cut into florets
- 2 tablespoons avocado oil
- 2 teaspoons taco seasoning
- 1 medium avocado
- ½ teaspoon garlic powder
- ¼ teaspoon black pepper
- ¼ teaspoon salt
- 2 tablespoons chopped red onion
- 2 teaspoons fresh squeezed lime juice
- ¼ cup chopped cilantro
- Eight 15-cm corn tortillas
- ½ cup cooked corn
- ½ cup shredded purple cabbage

Directions:

1. Preheat the air fryer to 200°C/390°F.
2. In a large bowl, toss the cauliflower with the avocado oil and taco seasoning. Set the metal trivet inside the air fryer basket and liberally spray with olive oil.
3. Place the cauliflower onto the trivet and cook for 10 minutes, shaking every 3 minutes to allow for an even char.
4. While the cauliflower is cooking, prepare the avocado sauce. In a medium bowl, mash the avocado; then mix in the garlic powder, pepper, salt, and onion. Stir in the

lime juice and cilantro; set aside.
5. Remove the cauliflower from the air fryer basket.
6. Place 1 tablespoon of avocado sauce in the middle of a tortilla, and top with corn, cabbage, and charred cauliflower. Repeat with the remaining tortillas. Serve immediately.

Variations & Ingredients Tips:

- Use broccoli, Brussels sprouts, or carrots instead of cauliflower for different veggie options.
- Add sliced radish, pickled onions, or queso fresco for extra toppings.
- Serve with salsa, hot sauce, or lime wedges on the side.

Per Serving (2 tacos): Calories: 380; Cholesterol: 0mg; Total Fat: 20g; Saturated Fat: 3g; Sodium: 520mg; Total Carbohydrates: 47g; Dietary Fiber: 11g; Total Sugars: 7g; Protein: 8g

Caprese-style Sandwiches

Servings: 2 | Prep Time: 10 Minutes | Cooking Time: 20 Minutes

Ingredients:

- 2 tbsp balsamic vinegar
- 4 sandwich bread slices
- 60 grams mozzarella shreds
- 3 tbsp pesto sauce
- 2 tomatoes, sliced
- 8 basil leaves
- 8 baby spinach leaves
- 2 tbsp olive oil

Directions:

1. Preheat air fryer at 175°C/350°F. Drizzle balsamic vinegar on the bottom of bread slices and smear with pesto sauce. Then, layer mozzarella cheese, tomatoes, baby spinach leaves and basil leaves on top. Add top bread slices. Rub the outside top and bottom of each sandwich with olive oil. Place them in the frying basket and Bake for 5 minutes, flipping once. Serve right away.

Variations & Ingredients Tips:

- Use ciabatta, focaccia, or sourdough bread for a rustic sandwich.
- Add sliced prosciutto or salami for a non-vegetarian version.
- Drizzle with extra balsamic glaze or olive oil before serving for added flavor.

Per Serving (1 sandwich): Calories: 450; Cholesterol: 25mg; Total Fat: 28g; Saturated Fat: 7g; Sodium: 670mg; Total Carbohydrates: 37g; Dietary Fiber: 4g; Total Sugars: 8g; Protein: 16g

Thai Peanut Veggie Burgers

Servings: 6 | Prep Time: 20 Minutes | Cooking Time: 14 Minutes

Ingredients:

- One 440-gram can cannellini beans
- 1 teaspoon minced garlic
- ¼ cup chopped onion
- 1 Thai chili pepper, sliced
- 2 tablespoons natural peanut butter
- ½ teaspoon black pepper
- ½ teaspoon salt
- ⅓ cup all-purpose flour (optional)
- ½ cup cooked quinoa
- 1 large carrot, grated
- 1 cup shredded red cabbage
- ¼ cup peanut dressing
- ¼ cup chopped cilantro
- 6 Hawaiian rolls
- 6 butterleaf lettuce leaves

Directions:

1. Preheat the air fryer to 180°C/350°F.
2. To a blender or food processor fitted with a metal blade, add the beans, garlic, onion, chili pepper, peanut butter, pepper, and salt. Pulse for 5 to 10 seconds. Do not over process. The mixture should be coarse, not smooth.
3. Remove from the blender or food processor and spoon into a large bowl. Mix in the cooked quinoa and carrots. At this point, the mixture should begin to hold together to form small patties. If the dough appears to be too sticky (meaning you likely processed a little too long), add the flour to hold the patties together.
4. Using a large spoon, form 8 equal patties out of the batter.
5. Liberally spray a metal trivet with olive oil spray and set in the air fryer basket. Place the patties into the basket, leaving enough space to be able to turn them with a spatula.
6. Cook for 7 minutes, flip, and cook another 7 minutes.
7. Remove from the heat and repeat with additional pat-

ties.
8. To serve, place the red cabbage in a bowl and toss with peanut dressing and cilantro. Place the veggie burger on a bun, and top with a slice of lettuce and cabbage slaw.

Variations & Ingredients Tips:

- Use chickpeas or black beans instead of cannellini beans.
- Substitute peanut butter with almond butter or sunflower seed butter.
- Add shredded beetroot or zucchini to the patty mixture.

Per Serving: Calories: 340; Total Fat: 11g; Saturated Fat: 2g; Sodium: 580mg; Total Carbohydrates: 50g; Dietary Fiber: 9g; Total Sugars: 8g; Protein: 13g

Balsamic Caprese Hasselback

Servings: 4 | Prep Time: 10 Minutes | Cooking Time: 15 Minutes

Ingredients:

- 4 tomatoes
- 12 fresh basil leaves
- 1 ball fresh mozzarella
- Salt and pepper to taste
- 1 tbsp olive oil
- 2 tsp balsamic vinegar
- 1 tbsp basil, torn

Directions:

1. Preheat air fryer to 165°C/325°F. Remove the bottoms from the tomatoes to create a flat surface. Make 4 even slices on each tomato, 3/4 of the way down. Slice the mozzarella and then cut into 12 pieces. Stuff 1 basil leaf and a piece of mozzarella into each slice. Sprinkle with salt and pepper. Place the stuffed tomatoes in the frying basket and Air Fry for 3 minutes. Transfer to a large serving plate. Drizzle with olive oil and balsamic vinegar and scatter the basil over. Serve and enjoy!

Variations & Ingredients Tips:

- Use cherry or grape tomatoes for bite-sized appetizers.
- Substitute mozzarella with provolone or fontina cheese for a different flavor.
- Add a drizzle of pesto or balsamic glaze for extra richness.

Per Serving: Calories: 160; Cholesterol: 25mg; Total Fat: 11g; Saturated Fat: 5g; Sodium: 220mg; Total Carbohydrates: 8g; Dietary Fiber: 2g; Total Sugars: 5g; Protein: 8g

Spiced Vegetable Galette

Servings: 4 | Prep Time: 15 Minutes | Cooking Time: 30 Minutes

Ingredients:

- ¼ cup cooked eggplant, chopped
- ¼ cup cooked zucchini, chopped
- 1 refrigerated pie crust
- 2 eggs
- ¼ cup milk
- Salt and pepper to taste
- 1 red chili, finely sliced
- ¼ cup tomato, chopped
- ½ cup shredded mozzarella cheese

Directions:

1. Preheat air fryer to 180°C/360°F.
2. In a baking dish, add the crust and press firmly. Trim off any excess edges. Poke a few holes.
3. Beat the eggs in a bowl. Stir in the milk, half of the cheese, eggplant, zucchini, tomato, red chili, salt, and pepper. Mix well.
4. Transfer the mixture to the baking dish and place in the air fryer.
5. Bake for 15 minutes or until firm and almost crusty. Slide the basket out and top with the remaining cheese.
6. Cook further for 5 minutes, or until golden brown. Let cool slightly and serve.

Variations & Ingredients Tips:

- Use puff pastry or phyllo dough instead of pie crust.
- Add sautéed onions, garlic, or mushrooms to the filling.
- Sprinkle with fresh herbs like basil, oregano, or thyme before serving.

Per Serving: Calories: 280; Total Fat: 18g; Saturated Fat: 7g; Sodium: 410mg; Total Carbohydrates: 21g; Dietary Fiber: 1g; Total Sugars: 4g; Protein: 9g

Spinach & Brie Frittata

Servings: 4 | Prep Time: 10 Minutes | Cooking Time: 25 Minutes

Ingredients:

- 5 eggs
- Salt and pepper to taste
- ½ cup baby spinach
- 1 shallot, diced
- 113 grams brie cheese, cubed
- 1 tomato, sliced

Directions:

1. Preheat air fryer to 160°C/320°F.
2. Whisk all ingredients, except for the tomato slices, in a bowl.
3. Transfer to a baking pan greased with olive oil and top with tomato slices.
4. Place the pan in the air fryer basket and Bake for 14 minutes.
5. Let cool for 5 minutes before slicing. Serve and enjoy!

Variations & Ingredients Tips:

- Substitute brie with goat cheese, feta, or cheddar.
- Add sliced mushrooms, bell peppers, or zucchini to the mix.
- Top with sliced avocado or a dollop of sour cream.

Per Serving: Calories: 220; Total Fat: 16g; Saturated Fat: 8g; Sodium: 320mg; Total Carbohydrates: 3g; Dietary Fiber: 0g; Total Sugars: 2g; Protein: 15g

Rigatoni With Roasted Onions, Fennel, Spinach And Lemon Pepper Ricotta

Servings: 2 | Prep Time: 10 Minutes | Cooking Time: 13 Minutes

Ingredients:

- 1 red onion, rough chopped into large chunks
- 2 teaspoons olive oil, divided
- 1 bulb fennel, sliced 0.6-cm thick
- ¾ cup ricotta cheese
- 1½ teaspoons finely chopped lemon zest, plus more for garnish
- 1 teaspoon lemon juice
- salt and freshly ground black pepper
- 227 grams dried rigatoni pasta
- 3 cups baby spinach leaves

Directions:

1. Bring a large stockpot of salted water to a boil on the stovetop and Preheat the air fryer to 200°C/400°F.
2. While the water is coming to a boil, toss the chopped onion in 1 teaspoon of olive oil and transfer to the air fryer basket. Air-fry at 200°C/400°F for 5 minutes.
3. Toss the sliced fennel with 1 teaspoon of olive oil and add this to the air fryer basket with the onions. Continue to air-fry at 200°C/400°F for 8 minutes, shaking the basket a few times during the cooking process.
4. Combine the ricotta cheese, lemon zest and juice, ¼ teaspoon of salt and freshly ground black pepper in a bowl and stir until smooth.
5. Add the dried rigatoni to the boiling water and cook according to the package directions. When the pasta is cooked al dente, reserve one cup of the pasta water and drain the pasta into a colander.
6. Place the spinach in a serving bowl and immediately transfer the hot pasta to the bowl, wilting the spinach. Add the roasted onions and fennel and toss together. Add a little pasta water to the dish if it needs moistening. Then, dollop the lemon pepper ricotta cheese on top and nestle it into the hot pasta. Garnish with more lemon zest if desired.

Variations & Ingredients Tips:

- Substitute fennel with sliced zucchini or eggplant.
- Use goat cheese or feta instead of ricotta for a tangy flavor.
- Add cooked chicken or shrimp for a non-vegetarian version.

Per Serving: Calories: 610; Total Fat: 19g; Saturated Fat: 9g; Sodium: 470mg; Total Carbohydrates: 89g; Dietary Fiber: 7g; Total Sugars: 8g; Protein: 24g

Lentil Fritters

Servings: 9 | Prep Time: 10 Minutes | Cooking Time: 12 Minutes

Ingredients:

- 1 cup cooked red lentils
- 1 cup riced cauliflower
- ½ medium zucchini, shredded (about 1 cup)
- ¼ cup finely chopped onion
- ¼ teaspoon salt
- ¼ teaspoon black pepper
- ½ teaspoon garlic powder
- ¼ teaspoon paprika
- 1 large egg
- ⅓ cup quinoa flour

Directions:

1. Preheat the air fryer to 190°C/370°F.
2. In a large bowl, mix the lentils, cauliflower, zucchini, onion, salt, pepper, garlic powder, and paprika. Mix in the egg and flour until a thick dough forms.
3. Using a large spoon, form the dough into 9 large fritters.
4. Liberally spray the air fryer basket with olive oil. Place the fritters into the basket, leaving space around each fritter so you can flip them.
5. Cook for 6 minutes, flip, and cook another 6 minutes.
6. Remove from the air fryer and repeat with the remaining fritters. Serve warm with desired sauce and sides.

Variations & Ingredients Tips:

- Use chickpea flour or almond meal instead of quinoa flour for a different flavor.
- Add shredded carrots or chopped bell peppers for extra veggie goodness.
- Serve with yogurt dip, hummus, or sweet chili sauce.

Per Serving: Calories: 60; Total Fat: 1.5g; Saturated Fat: 0g; Sodium: 90mg; Total Carbohydrates: 8g; Dietary Fiber: 2g; Total Sugars: 1g; Protein: 3g

Sweet Roasted Carrots

Servings: 4 | Prep Time: 10 Minutes | Cooking Time: 25 Minutes

Ingredients:

- 6 carrots, cut into 1-cm pieces
- 2 tbsp butter, melted
- 2 tbsp parsley, chopped
- 1 tsp honey

Directions:

1. Preheat air fryer to 200°C/390°F.
2. Add carrots to a baking pan and pour over butter, honey, and 2-3 tbsp of water. Mix well.
3. Transfer the carrots to the greased air fryer basket and Roast for 12 minutes, shaking the basket once.
4. Sprinkle with parsley and serve warm.

Variations & Ingredients Tips:

- Toss carrots with cumin, paprika, or za'atar spice blend before roasting.
- Drizzle with tahini sauce or yogurt dressing after air frying.
- Add parsnips, beets, or sweet potatoes along with the carrots.

Per Serving: Calories: 100; Total Fat: 6g; Saturated Fat: 3.5g; Sodium: 110mg; Total Carbohydrates: 12g; Dietary Fiber: 3g; Total Sugars: 7g; Protein: 1g

Roasted Vegetable Thai Green Curry

Servings: 4 | Prep Time: 15 Minutes | Cooking Time: 16 Minutes

Ingredients:

- 1 (400-ml) can coconut milk
- 3 tablespoons green curry paste
- 1 tablespoon soy sauce*
- 1 tablespoon rice wine vinegar
- 1 teaspoon sugar
- 1 teaspoon minced fresh ginger
- ½ onion, chopped
- 3 carrots, sliced
- 1 red bell pepper, chopped
- olive oil
- 10 stalks of asparagus, cut into 5-cm pieces
- 3 cups broccoli florets
- basmati rice for serving
- fresh cilantro
- crushed red pepper flakes (optional)

Directions:

1. Combine the coconut milk, green curry paste, soy sauce, rice wine vinegar, sugar and ginger in a medium saucepan and bring to a boil on the stovetop. Reduce the heat and simmer for 20 minutes while you cook the vegetables. Set aside.
2. Preheat the air fryer to 200°C/400°F.
3. Toss the onion, carrots, and red pepper together with a little olive oil and transfer the vegetables to the air fryer basket. Air-fry at 200°C/400°F for 10 minutes, shaking the basket a few times during the cooking process.
4. Add the asparagus and broccoli florets and air-fry for an additional 6 minutes, again shaking the basket for even cooking.
5. When the vegetables are cooked to your liking, toss them with the green curry sauce and serve in bowls over basmati rice. Garnish with fresh chopped cilantro and crushed red pepper flakes.

Variations & Ingredients Tips:

- ▸ Use yellow or red curry paste for a different flavor profile.
- ▸ Add cubed tofu or tempeh for extra protein.
- ▸ Serve with quinoa or rice noodles instead of basmati rice.

Per Serving: Calories: 420; Total Fat: 32g; Saturated Fat: 25g; Sodium: 680mg; Total Carbohydrates: 30g; Dietary Fiber: 7g; Total Sugars: 8g; Protein: 8g

Pesto Pepperoni Pizza Bread

Servings: 4 | Prep Time: 10 Minutes | Cooking Time: 25 Minutes

Ingredients:

- 2 eggs, beaten
- 2 tbsp flour
- 2 tbsp cassava flour
- 1/3 cup whipping cream
- ¼ cup chopped pepperoni
- 1/3 cup grated mozzarella
- 2 tsp Italian seasoning
- ½ tsp baking powder
- ⅛ tsp salt
- 3 tsp grated Parmesan cheese
- ½ cup pesto

Directions:

1. Preheat air fryer to 150°C/300°F.
2. Combine all ingredients, except for the Parmesan and pesto sauce, in a bowl until mixed.
3. Pour the batter into a 25-cm pizza pan. Place it in the air fryer basket and Bake for 20 minutes.
4. After, sprinkle Parmesan on top and cook for 1 minute.
5. Let chill for 5 minutes before slicing. Serve with warmed pesto sauce.

Variations & Ingredients Tips:

- ▸ Use spinach or kale pesto for a greener taste and color.
- ▸ Add sun-dried tomatoes or olives for a Mediterranean flair.
- ▸ Sprinkle with red pepper flakes for some heat.

Per Serving: Calories: 320; Total Fat: 24g; Saturated Fat: 10g; Sodium: 510mg; Total Carbohydrates: 13g; Dietary Fiber: 1g; Total Sugars: 1g; Protein: 12g

Powerful Jackfruit Fritters

Servings: 4 | Prep Time: 20 Minutes | Cooking Time: 30 Minutes

Ingredients:

- 1 can jackfruit, chopped
- 1 egg, beaten
- 1 tbsp Dijon mustard
- 1 tbsp mayonnaise
- 1 tbsp prepared horseradish
- 2 tbsp grated yellow onion
- 2 tbsp chopped parsley
- 2 tbsp chopped nori
- 2 tbsp flour
- 1 tbsp Cajun seasoning
- ¼ tsp garlic powder
- ¼ tsp salt
- 2 lemon wedges

Directions:

1. In a bowl, combine jackfruit, egg, mustard, mayonnaise, horseradish, onion, parsley, nori, flour, Cajun seasoning, garlic, and salt. Let chill in the fridge for 15 minutes.
2. Preheat air fryer to 180°C/350°F.
3. Divide the mixture into 12 balls. Place them in the air fryer basket and Air Fry for 10 minutes.
4. Serve with lemon wedges.

Variations & Ingredients Tips:

- ▸ Substitute jackfruit with canned artichoke hearts or hearts of palm.
- ▸ Use Old Bay seasoning instead of Cajun for a different spice profile.
- ▸ Serve with tartar sauce or spicy remoulade.

Per Serving: Calories: 120; Total Fat: 5g; Saturated Fat: 1g; Sodium: 730mg; Total Carbohydrates: 16g; Dietary Fiber: 3g; Total Sugars: 6g; Protein: 4g

Roasted Vegetable, Brown Rice And Black Bean Burrito

Servings: 2 | Prep Time: 10 Minutes | Cooking Time: 20 Minutes

Ingredients:

- 1/2 zucchini, sliced 0.6 cm thick

- 1/2 red onion, sliced
- 1 yellow bell pepper, sliced
- 2 teaspoons olive oil
- Salt and freshly ground black pepper
- 2 burrito size flour tortillas
- 1 cup grated pepper jack cheese
- 1/2 cup cooked brown rice
- 1/2 cup canned black beans, drained and rinsed
- 1/4 teaspoon ground cumin
- 1 tablespoon chopped fresh cilantro
- Fresh salsa, guacamole and sour cream, for serving

Directions:

1. Preheat air fryer to 200°C/400°F.
2. Toss veggies with oil, salt and pepper. Air fry 12-15 mins, shaking occasionally until tender.
3. Lay out tortillas and sprinkle half the cheese in the center.
4. Mix rice, beans, cumin, cilantro and season. Divide between tortillas.
5. Top with roasted veggies and remaining cheese. Roll up burritos.
6. Brush or spray outsides with oil. Air fry at 180°C/360°F for 8 mins, flipping halfway.
7. Serve warm with salsa, guacamole and sour cream.

Variations & Ingredients Tips:

- Use whole wheat or spinach tortillas.
- Substitute black beans with pinto or kidney beans.
- Add sautéed mushrooms or diced avocado to filling.

Per Serving: Calories: 631; Total Fat: 28g; Saturated Fat: 13g; Sodium: 934mg; Total Carbohydrates: 72g; Dietary Fiber: 13g; Total Sugars: 6g; Protein: 25g

Tex-mex Potatoes With Avocado Dressing

Servings: 2 | Prep Time: 20 Minutes | Cooking Time: 60 Minutes

Ingredients:

- ¼ cup chopped parsley, dill, cilantro, chives
- ¼ cup yogurt
- ½ avocado, diced
- 2 tbsp milk
- 2 tsp lemon juice
- ½ tsp lemon zest
- 1 green onion, chopped
- 2 cloves garlic, quartered
- Salt and pepper to taste
- 2 tsp olive oil
- 2 russet potatoes, scrubbed and perforated with a fork
- 1 cup steamed broccoli florets
- ½ cup canned white beans

Directions:

1. In a food processor, blend the yogurt, avocado, milk, lemon juice, lemon zest, green onion, garlic, parsley, dill, cilantro, chives, salt and pepper until smooth. Transfer it to a small bowl and let chill the dressing covered in the fridge until ready to use.
2. Preheat air fryer at 200°C/400°F. Rub olive oil over both potatoes and sprinkle with salt and pepper. Place them in the air fryer basket and Bake for 45 minutes, flipping at 30 minutes mark.
3. Let cool onto a cutting board for 5 minutes until cool enough to handle. Cut each potato lengthwise into slices and pinch ends together to open up each slice.
4. Stuff broccoli and beans into potatoes and put them back into the basket, and cook for 3 more minutes.
5. Drizzle avocado dressing over and serve.

Variations & Ingredients Tips:

- Substitute russet potatoes with sweet potatoes or yams.
- Use cauliflower florets or asparagus instead of broccoli.
- Add cooked quinoa or brown rice to the stuffing.

Per Serving: Calories: 450; Total Fat: 18g; Saturated Fat: 3g; Sodium: 250mg; Total Carbohydrates: 64g; Dietary Fiber: 12g; Total Sugars: 5g; Protein: 14g

Fried Rice With Curried Tofu

Servings: 4 | Prep Time: 10 Minutes | Cooking Time: 25 Minutes

Ingredients:

- 225g extra-firm tofu, cubed
- 1/2 cup canned coconut milk
- 2 tsp red curry paste
- 2 cloves garlic, minced
- 1 tbsp avocado oil
- 1 tbsp coconut oil
- 2 cups cooked rice

- 1 tbsp turmeric powder
- Salt and pepper to taste
- 4 lime wedges
- 1/4 cup chopped cilantro

Directions:

1. Preheat air fryer to 175°C/350°F.
2. Combine tofu, coconut milk, curry paste, garlic, and avocado oil in a bowl. Pour the mixture into a baking pan. Place the pan in the frying basket and Air Fry for 10 minutes, stirring once.
3. Melt the coconut oil in a skillet over medium heat. Add in rice, turmeric powder, salt, and black pepper, and cook for 2 minutes or until heated through.
4. Divide the cooked rice between 4 medium bowls and top with tofu mixture and sauce. Top with cilantro and lime wedges to serve.

Variations & Ingredients Tips:

- Use brown rice or quinoa for extra fiber and nutrients.
- Add diced bell peppers or carrots for extra veggies.
- Top with cashews or peanuts for a crunchy texture.

Per Serving: Calories: 330; Total Fat: 21g; Saturated Fat: 9g; Sodium: 125mg; Total Carbs: 27g; Dietary Fiber: 3g; Total Sugars: 1g; Protein: 11g

Pinto Bean Casserole

Servings: 2 | Prep Time: 5 Minutes | Cooking Time: 15 Minutes

Ingredients:

- 1 can pinto beans
- ¼ cup tomato sauce
- 2 tbsp cornstarch
- 2 garlic cloves, minced
- ½ tsp dried oregano
- ½ tsp cumin
- 1 tsp smoked paprika
- Salt and pepper to taste

Directions:

1. Preheat air fryer to 200°C/390°F.
2. Stir the beans, tomato sauce, cornstarch, garlic, oregano, cumin, smoked paprika, salt, and pepper in a bowl until combined.
3. Pour the bean mix into a greased baking pan.
4. Bake in the fryer for 4 minutes. Remove, stir, and Bake for 4 minutes or until the mix is thick and heated through.
5. Serve hot.

Variations & Ingredients Tips:

- Top with shredded cheese, sour cream, and chopped cilantro.
- Add diced bell peppers and onions for extra veggies.
- Use black beans or kidney beans for variation.

Per Serving: Calories: 280; Total Fat: 1.5g; Saturated Fat: 0g; Sodium: 980mg; Total Carbohydrates: 52g; Dietary Fiber: 15g; Total Sugars: 2g; Protein: 15g

Cheddar Stuffed Portobellos With Salsa

Servings: 4 | Prep Time: 10 Minutes | Cooking Time: 20 Minutes

Ingredients:

- 8 portobello mushrooms
- 1/3 cup salsa
- ½ cup shredded cheddar
- 2 tbsp cilantro, chopped

Directions:

1. Preheat air fryer to 190°C/370°F. Remove the mushroom stems. Divide the salsa between the caps. Top with cheese and sprinkle with cilantro. Place the mushrooms in the greased frying basket and Bake for 8-10 minutes. Let cool slightly, then serve.

Variations & Ingredients Tips:

- Substitute cheddar with mozzarella, pepper jack, or a vegan cheese alternative.
- Add diced bell peppers, onions, or jalapeños to the salsa for extra veggies.
- Serve with sour cream, guacamole, or extra salsa on the side.

Per Serving (2 mushrooms): Calories: 120; Cholesterol: 15mg; Total Fat: 7g; Saturated Fat: 4g; Sodium: 320mg; Total Carbohydrates: 8g; Dietary Fiber: 2g; Total Sugars: 3g; Protein: 8g

Thyme Meatless Patties

Servings: 3 | Prep Time: 10 Minutes | Cooking

Time: 25 Minutes

Ingredients:

- ½ cup oat flour
- 1 tsp allspice
- ½ tsp ground thyme
- 1 tsp maple syrup
- ½ tsp liquid smoke
- 1 tsp balsamic vinegar

Directions:

1. Preheat air fryer to 200°C/400°F.
2. Mix the oat flour, allspice, thyme, maple syrup, liquid smoke, balsamic vinegar, and 2 tbsp of water in a bowl.
3. Make 6 patties out of the mixture. Place them onto a parchment paper and flatten them to 1-cm thick. Grease the patties with cooking spray.
4. Grill for 12 minutes until crispy, turning once.
5. Serve warm.

Variations & Ingredients Tips:

- Add finely chopped walnuts, sunflower seeds, or pumpkin seeds for crunch.
- Use date syrup or agave nectar instead of maple syrup.
- Serve with a dipping sauce like BBQ, ketchup, or sweet chili sauce.

Per Serving: Calories: 110; Total Fat: 2g; Saturated Fat: 0g; Sodium: 5mg; Total Carbohydrates: 19g; Dietary Fiber: 2g; Total Sugars: 4g; Protein: 3g

Vietnamese Gingered Tofu

Servings: 4 | Prep Time: 10 Minutes | Cooking Time: 25 Minutes

Ingredients:

- 1 package extra-firm tofu, cubed
- 4 tsp shoyu (soy sauce)
- 1 tsp onion powder
- 1/2 tsp garlic powder
- 1/2 tsp ginger powder
- 1/2 tsp turmeric powder
- Black pepper to taste
- 2 tbsp nutritional yeast
- 1 tsp dried rosemary
- 1 tsp dried dill
- 2 tsp cornstarch
- 2 tsp sunflower oil

Directions:

1. Sprinkle the tofu with shoyu and toss to coat.
2. Add the onion, garlic, ginger, turmeric, and pepper. Gently toss to coat.
3. Add the yeast, rosemary, dill, and cornstarch. Toss to coat.
4. Dribble with the oil and toss again.
5. Preheat air fryer to 200°C/390°F. Spray the basket with oil.
6. Put the tofu in the basket and Bake for 7 minutes.
7. Remove, shake gently, and cook for another 7 minutes or until crispy and golden.
8. Serve warm.

Variations & Ingredients Tips:

- Use tamari or coconut aminos instead of soy sauce.
- Add chili garlic sauce or sriracha for a spicy kick.
- Toss with chopped scallions before serving.

Per Serving: Calories: 132; Total Fat: 7g; Saturated Fat: 1g; Sodium: 514mg; Total Carbohydrates: 8g; Dietary Fiber: 2g; Total Sugars: 1g; Protein: 13g

Vegetable Side Dishes Recipes

Simple Zucchini Ribbons

Servings: 4 | Prep Time: 10 Minutes | Cooking Time: 15 Minutes

Ingredients:

- 2 zucchini
- 2 teaspoons butter, melted
- ¼ teaspoon garlic powder
- ¼ teaspoon chili flakes
- 8 cherry tomatoes, halved
- Salt and pepper to taste

Directions:

1. Preheat air fryer to 135°C/275°F.
2. Cut the zucchini into ribbons with a vegetable peeler.
3. Mix them with butter, garlic, chili flakes, salt, and pepper in a bowl.
4. Transfer to the frying basket and Air Fry for 2 minutes.
5. Toss and add the cherry tomatoes. Cook for another 2 minutes.
6. Serve.

Variations & Ingredients Tips:

- Add some grated Parmesan cheese or feta cheese for a salty and tangy flavor.
- Swap out the cherry tomatoes for sun-dried tomatoes or roasted red peppers for a different flavor profile.
- Use olive oil instead of butter for a healthier version.

Per Serving: Calories: 45; Total Fat: 2.5g; Saturated Fat: 1.5g; Cholesterol: 5mg; Sodium: 25mg; Total Carbs: 4g; Fiber: 1g; Sugars: 3g; Protein: 1g

Rich Spinach Chips

Servings: 4 | Prep Time: 5 Minutes | Cooking Time: 20 Minutes

Ingredients:

- 284g spinach
- 2 tbsp lemon juice
- 2 tbsp olive oil
- Salt and pepper to taste
- 1/2 tsp garlic powder
- 1/2 tsp onion powder

Directions:

1. Preheat air fryer to 177°C/350°F.
2. Place spinach in a bowl and drizzle with lemon juice and olive oil. Massage with your hands.
3. Season spinach with salt, pepper, garlic powder and onion powder. Toss gently to coat.
4. Arrange spinach in a single layer in the air fryer basket.
5. Bake for 3 minutes, shake basket and bake 1-3 minutes more until crispy.
6. Let cool completely before serving.

Variations & Ingredients Tips:

- Use kale, beet greens or chard instead of spinach.
- Add parmesan, nutritional yeast or ranch seasoning before baking.
- Bake at a lower temp for chewier chips.

Per Serving: Calories: 61; Total Fat: 5g; Saturated Fat: 1g; Cholesterol: 0mg; Sodium: 46mg; Total Carbohydrates: 4g; Dietary Fiber: 3g; Total Sugars: 1g; Protein: 2g

Glazed Carrots

Servings: 4 | Prep Time: 5 Minutes | Cooking Time: 10 Minutes

Ingredients:

- 2 teaspoons honey
- 1 teaspoon orange juice
- 1/2 teaspoon grated orange rind
- 1/8 teaspoon ginger
- 454g baby carrots
- 2 teaspoons olive oil
- 1/4 teaspoon salt

Directions:

1. Combine honey, orange juice, grated rind, and ginger in a small bowl and set aside.
2. Toss the carrots, oil, and salt together to coat well and pour them into the air fryer basket.
3. Cook at 200°C/390°F for 5 minutes. Shake basket to stir a little and cook for 4 minutes more, until carrots are barely tender.
4. Pour carrots into air fryer baking pan.
5. Stir the honey mixture to combine well, pour glaze over carrots, and stir to coat.
6. Cook at 182°C/360°F for 1 minute or just until heated through.

Variations & Ingredients Tips:

- For extra flavor, add a pinch of cinnamon or nutmeg to the glaze.
- Swap orange juice for lemon or lime juice.
- Use maple syrup instead of honey.

Per Serving: Calories: 90; Total Fat: 2.5g; Saturated Fat: 0g; Cholesterol: 0mg; Sodium: 200mg; Total Carbohydrates: 16g; Dietary Fiber: 3g; Total Sugars: 11g; Protein: 1g

Brown Rice And Goat Cheese Croquettes

Servings: 3 | Prep Time: 15 Minutes | Cooking Time: 8 Minutes

Ingredients:

- ¾ cup Water
- 6 tablespoons Raw medium-grain brown rice, such as brown Arborio
- ½ cup Shredded carrot
- ¼ cup Walnut pieces
- 3 tablespoons (about 43g) Soft goat cheese
- 1 tablespoon Pasteurized egg substitute, such as Egg Beaters (gluten-free, if a concern)
- ¼ teaspoon Dried thyme
- ¼ teaspoon Table salt
- ¼ teaspoon Ground black pepper
- Olive oil spray

Directions:

1. Combine the water, rice, and carrots in a small saucepan set over medium-high heat. Bring to a boil, stirring occasionally. Cover, reduce the heat to very low, and simmer very slowly for 45 minutes, or until the water has been absorbed and the rice is tender. Set aside, covered, for 10 minutes.
2. Scrape the contents of the saucepan into a food processor. Cool for 10 minutes.
3. Preheat the air fryer to 200°C/400°F.
4. Put the nuts, cheese, egg substitute, thyme, salt, and pepper into the food processor. Cover and pulse to a coarse paste, stopping the machine at least once to scrape down the inside of the canister.
5. Uncover the food processor; scrape down and remove the blade. Using wet, clean hands, form the mixture into two 10cm-diameter patties for a small batch, three 10cm-diameter patties for a medium batch, or four 10cm-diameter patties for a large one. Generously coat both sides of the patties with olive oil spray.
6. Set the patties in the basket with as much air space between them as possible. Air-fry undisturbed for 8 minutes, or until brown and crisp.
7. Use a nonstick-safe spatula to transfer the croquettes to a wire rack. Cool for 5 minutes before serving.

Variations & Ingredients Tips:

- Substitute different grains like quinoa or farro for the brown rice.
- Add finely chopped spinach or kale to the mixture.
- Serve with a yogurt dill sauce for dipping.

Per Serving: Calories: 225; Total Fat: 10g; Saturated Fat: 3g; Cholesterol: 5mg; Sodium: 330mg; Total Carbs: 27g; Fiber: 3g; Sugars: 2g; Protein: 8g

Garlicky Bell Pepper Mix

Servings: 4 | Prep Time: 10 Minutes | Cooking Time: 30 Minutes

Ingredients:

- 2 tbsp vegetable oil
- ½ tsp dried cilantro
- 1 red bell pepper
- 1 yellow bell pepper
- 1 orange bell pepper
- 1 green bell pepper
- Salt and pepper to taste
- 1 head garlic

Directions:

1. Preheat air fryer to 165°C/330°F.
2. Slice the peppers into 5cm strips. Transfer to a bowl with 1 tbsp vegetable oil and toss to coat. Season with cilantro, salt, and pepper.

3. Cut the top off garlic head and place cut-side up on an oiled aluminum foil square. Drizzle with oil and wrap completely.
4. Roast the wrapped garlic for 15 minutes. Then add pepper strips and roast 6-8 more minutes until peppers are tender and garlic is soft.
5. Transfer peppers to a dish. Unwrap garlic carefully and squeeze cloves into the pepper dish once cooled.
6. Serve.

Variations & Ingredients Tips:

- Add sliced onions or mushrooms to the mix.
- Sprinkle with grated parmesan before serving.
- Substitute balsamic vinegar for some of the oil.

Per Serving: Calories: 95; Total Fat: 7g; Saturated Fat: 1g; Cholesterol: 0mg; Sodium: 10mg; Total Carbs: 8g; Fiber: 2g; Sugars: 3g; Protein: 1g

Spiced Pumpkin Wedges

Servings: 4 | Prep Time: 10 Minutes | Cooking Time: 35 Minutes

Ingredients:

- 625 ml pumpkin, cubed
- 2 tablespoons olive oil
- Salt and pepper to taste
- ¼ teaspoon pumpkin pie spice
- 1 tablespoon thyme
- 30 g grated Parmesan

Directions:

1. Preheat air fryer to 180°C/360°F.
2. Put the cubed pumpkin with olive oil, salt, pumpkin pie spice, black pepper, and thyme in a bowl and stir until the pumpkin is well coated.
3. Pour this mixture into the frying basket and Roast for 18-20 minutes, stirring once.
4. Sprinkle the pumpkin with grated Parmesan.
5. Serve and enjoy!

Variations & Ingredients Tips:

- Use different types of winter squash, such as butternut squash or acorn squash, for a variety of flavors and textures.
- Add some chopped pecans or walnuts for a crunchy texture and nutty flavor.
- For a sweeter version, drizzle the pumpkin wedges with honey or maple syrup before serving.

Per Serving: Calories: 130; Total Fat: 8g; Saturated Fat: 2g; Cholesterol: 5mg; Sodium: 180mg; Total Carbs: 12g; Fiber: 2g; Sugars: 3g; Protein: 4g

Citrusy Brussels Sprouts

Servings: 4 | Prep Time: 10 Minutes | Cooking Time: 15 Minutes

Ingredients:

- 454g Brussels sprouts, quartered
- 1 clementine, cut into rings
- 2 garlic cloves, minced
- 1 tbsp olive oil
- 1 tbsp butter, melted
- ½ tsp salt

Directions:

1. Preheat air fryer to 182°C/360°F.
2. Add the quartered Brussels sprouts with the garlic, olive oil, butter and salt in a bowl and toss until well coated.
3. Pour the Brussels sprouts into the air fryer, top with the clementine slices.
4. Roast for 10 minutes.
5. Remove from the air fryer and set the clementines aside.
6. Toss the Brussels sprouts and serve.

Variations & Ingredients Tips:

- Use orange or grapefruit sections instead of clementine.
- Add sliced almonds or pecans for crunch.
- Drizzle with balsamic glaze before serving.

Per Serving: Calories: 130; Total Fat: 8g; Saturated Fat: 2g; Cholesterol: 5mg; Sodium: 290mg; Total Carbs: 13g; Fiber: 5g; Sugars: 3g; Protein: 4g

Roasted Yellow Squash And Onions

Servings: 3 | Prep Time: 10 Minutes | Cooking Time: 20 Minutes

Ingredients:

- 1 medium (20cm) yellow or summer squash, cut into 1.25cm rounds
- 1 1/2 cups chopped yellow or white onion (1

- large)
- 3/4 teaspoon table salt
- 1/4 teaspoon ground cumin (optional)
- Olive oil spray
- 1 1/2 tablespoons lemon or lime juice

Directions:

1. Preheat air fryer to 190°C/375°F.
2. Toss squash rounds, onion, salt and cumin (if using) in a bowl.
3. Lightly coat veggies all over with olive oil spray.
4. When preheated, spread veggies in an even layer in air fryer basket.
5. Air fry for 20 minutes, tossing gently once, until tender and lightly browned.
6. Transfer to a bowl and toss with lemon or lime juice.
7. Serve warm or at room temperature.

Variations & Ingredients Tips:

- Add diced bell peppers or zucchini to the mix.
- Use balsamic or red wine vinegar instead of citrus juice.
- Sprinkle with parmesan or feta cheese before serving.

Per Serving: Calories: 60; Total Fat: 1g; Saturated Fat: 0g; Cholesterol: 0mg; Sodium: 590mg; Total Carbohydrates: 12g; Dietary Fiber: 3g; Total Sugars: 6g; Protein: 2g

Corn On The Cob

Servings: 4 | Prep Time: 5 Minutes | Cooking Time: 12 Minutes

Ingredients:

- 2 large ears fresh corn
- Olive oil for misting
- Salt (optional)

Directions:

1. Shuck corn, remove silks, and wash.
2. Cut or break each ear in half crosswise.
3. Spray corn with olive oil.
4. Cook at 198°C/390°F for 12 minutes or until browned as much as you like.
5. Serve plain or with coarsely ground salt.

Variations & Ingredients Tips:

- Brush with garlic butter or herb butter before cooking.
- Sprinkle with chili lime seasoning after cooking.
- Add grated parmesan or cotija cheese.

Per Serving: Calories: 120; Total Fat: 3g; Saturated Fat: 0g; Cholesterol: 0mg; Sodium: 10mg; Total Carbs: 22g; Fiber: 3g; Sugars: 5g; Protein: 4g

Hasselbacks

Servings: 4 | Prep Time: 10 Minutes | Cooking Time: 41 Minutes

Ingredients:

- 2 large (454g each) potatoes
- Oil for misting or cooking spray
- Salt, pepper, and garlic powder
- 43g sharp cheddar cheese, sliced very thin
- 1/4 cup chopped green onions
- 2 strips turkey bacon, cooked and crumbled
- Light sour cream for serving (optional)

Directions:

1. Preheat air fryer to 199°C/390°F.
2. Scrub potatoes. Cut thin vertical slices 6mm thick crosswise about three-quarters of the way down so that bottom of potato remains intact.
3. Fan potatoes slightly to separate slices. Mist with oil and sprinkle with salt, pepper, and garlic powder to taste.
4. Place potatoes in air fryer basket and cook for 40 minutes or until centers test done when pierced with a fork.
5. Top potatoes with cheese slices and cook for 30 seconds to 1 minute to melt cheese.
6. Cut each potato in half crosswise, and sprinkle with green onions and crumbled bacon. If desired, add a dollop of sour cream before serving.

Variations & Ingredients Tips:

- Mix shredded cheese into the seasoning before baking for extra cheesy potatoes.
- Brush with garlic butter before serving.
- Top with chives, bacon bits, sour cream or salsa.

Per Serving: Calories: 280; Total Fat: 6g; Saturated Fat: 3g; Cholesterol: 20mg; Sodium: 280mg; Total Carbohydrates: 48g; Dietary Fiber: 5g; Total Sugars: 2g; Protein: 10g

Smashed Fried Baby Potatoes

Servings: 3 | Prep Time: 30 Minutes | Cooking Time: 18 Minutes

Ingredients:

- 680 g baby red or baby Yukon gold potatoes
- 60 g butter, melted
- 1 teaspoon olive oil
- ½ teaspoon paprika
- 1 teaspoon dried parsley
- Salt and freshly ground black pepper
- 2 scallions, finely chopped

Directions:

1. Bring a large pot of salted water to a boil. Add the potatoes and boil for 18 minutes or until the potatoes are fork-tender.
2. Drain the potatoes and transfer them to a cutting board to cool slightly. Spray or brush the bottom of a drinking glass with a little oil. Smash or flatten the potatoes by pressing the glass down on each potato slowly. Try not to completely flatten the potato or smash it so hard that it breaks apart.
3. Combine the melted butter, olive oil, paprika, and parsley together.
4. Preheat the air fryer to 200°C/400°F.
5. Spray the bottom of the air fryer basket with oil and transfer one layer of the smashed potatoes into the basket. Brush with some of the butter mixture and season generously with salt and freshly ground black pepper.
6. Air-fry at 200°C/400°F for 10 minutes. Carefully flip the potatoes over and air-fry for an additional 8 minutes until crispy and lightly browned.
7. Keep the potatoes warm in a 75°C/170°F oven or tent with aluminum foil while you cook the second batch.
8. Sprinkle minced scallions over the potatoes and serve warm.

Variations & Ingredients Tips:

- Use garlic powder or onion powder instead of paprika for a different flavor profile.
- Top the potatoes with shredded cheddar cheese or crumbled bacon for a more indulgent side dish.
- Serve the potatoes with sour cream or ranch dressing for dipping.

Per Serving: Calories: 280; Total Fat: 14g; Saturated Fat: 8g; Cholesterol: 35mg; Sodium: 170mg; Total Carbs: 35g; Fiber: 4g; Sugars: 2g; Protein: 4g

Shoestring Butternut Squash Fries

Servings: 3 | Prep Time: 10 Minutes | Cooking Time: 16 Minutes

Ingredients:

- 567g spiralized butternut squash strands
- Vegetable oil spray
- Coarse sea salt or kosher salt to taste

Directions:

1. Preheat air fryer to 190°C/375°F.
2. Place squash strands in a bowl and coat generously with vegetable oil spray, tossing several times to evenly coat.
3. When preheated, spread squash strands in an even layer in the air fryer basket.
4. Air fry for 16 minutes, tossing and rearranging every 4 minutes, until lightly browned and crisp.
5. Transfer squash fries to a bowl and season with salt to taste.
6. Serve hot.

Variations & Ingredients Tips:

- Use sweet potato or beet spirals instead of squash.
- Toss with cajun seasoning, ranch powder or grated parmesan before serving.
- Bake at 204°C/400°F for a crispier fry.

Per Serving: Calories: 92; Total Fat: 1g; Saturated Fat: 0g; Cholesterol: 0mg; Sodium: 75mg; Total Carbs: 20g; Dietary Fiber: 4g; Total Sugars: 4g; Protein: 2g

Mediterranean Roasted Vegetables

Servings: 4 | Prep Time: 10 Minutes | Cooking Time: 30 Minutes

Ingredients:

- 1 red bell pepper, cut into chunks
- 1 cup sliced mushrooms
- 1 cup green beans, diced
- 1 zucchini, sliced
- 1/3 cup diced red onion
- 3 garlic cloves, sliced
- 2 tbsp olive oil
- 1 tsp rosemary

- 1/2 tsp flaked sea salt

Directions:

1. Preheat air fryer to 180°C/350°F.
2. Add the bell pepper, mushrooms, green beans, red onion, zucchini, rosemary, and garlic to a bowl and mix.
3. Spritz with olive oil and stir until well-coated.
4. Put the veggies in the frying basket and air fry for 14-18 minutes until crispy and softened.
5. Serve sprinkled with flaked sea salt.

Variations & Ingredients Tips:

- Add diced eggplant or cherry tomatoes.
- Use balsamic vinegar instead of olive oil.
- Toss with fresh basil or parmesan after cooking.

Per Serving: Calories: 88; Total Fat: 5g; Saturated Fat: 1g; Cholesterol: 0mg; Sodium: 106mg; Total Carbohydrates: 10g; Dietary Fiber: 3g; Total Sugars: 5g; Protein: 3g

Roasted Ratatouille Vegetables

Cooking Time: 15 Minutes | Prep Time: 10 Minutes | Servings: 2

Ingredients:

- 1 baby or Japanese eggplant, cut into 3.5cm cubes
- 1 red pepper, cut into 2.5cm chunks
- 1 yellow pepper, cut into 2.5cm chunks
- 1 zucchini, cut into 2.5cm chunks
- 1 garlic clove, minced
- 1/2 teaspoon dried basil
- 1 tablespoon olive oil
- Salt and freshly ground black pepper
- 1/4 cup sliced sun-dried tomatoes in oil
- 2 tablespoons chopped fresh basil

Directions:

1. Preheat air fryer to 200°C/400°F.
2. Toss eggplant, peppers, zucchini, garlic, dried basil, olive oil, salt and pepper in a bowl.
3. Air fry veggies at 200°C/400°F for 15 minutes, shaking basket a few times.
4. When tender, toss immediately with sun-dried tomatoes and fresh basil.
5. Serve.

Variations & Ingredients Tips:

- Add halved cherry tomatoes before roasting.
- Drizzle with balsamic glaze or lemon juice after roasting.
- Sprinkle with parmesan or feta cheese.

Per Serving: Calories: 156; Total Fat: 11g; Saturated Fat: 1g; Cholesterol: 0mg; Sodium: 69mg; Total Carbohydrates: 13g; Dietary Fiber: 5g; Total Sugars: 8g; Protein: 3g

Honey-roasted Parsnips

Servings: 3 | Prep Time: 10 Minutes | Cooking Time: 23 Minutes

Ingredients:

- 680g medium parsnips, peeled
- Olive oil spray
- 1 tablespoon honey
- 1 1/2 teaspoons water
- 1/4 teaspoon table salt

Directions:

1. Preheat the air fryer to 177°C/350°F.
2. If the thick end of a parsnip is more than 1.25cm in diameter, cut just below where it swells to the large end, then slice the large section in half lengthwise.
3. If parsnips are larger than the basket, trim off the thin end so they fit. Generously coat all sides with olive oil spray.
4. When machine is at temperature, set parsnips in basket with space between them. Air fry undisturbed for 20 minutes.
5. Whisk the honey, water, and salt in a small bowl until smooth. Brush this mixture over the parsnips.
6. Air fry undisturbed for 3 minutes more, or until the glaze is lightly browned.
7. Use tongs to transfer parsnips to a wire rack or serving platter. Cool for a couple of minutes before serving.

Variations & Ingredients Tips:

- Add cinnamon or nutmeg to the glaze for warmth.
- Substitute maple syrup for the honey.
- Toss with chopped parsley or thyme after roasting.

Per Serving: Calories: 131; Total Fat: 0.2g; Saturated Fat: 0g; Cholesterol: 0mg; Sodium: 156mg; Total Carbs: 31g; Dietary Fiber: 7g; Total Sugars: 14g; Protein: 2g

Buttered Garlic Broccolini

Servings: 2 | Prep Time: 10 Minutes | Cooking Time: 20 Minutes

Ingredients:

- 1 bunch broccolini
- 2 tbsp butter, cubed
- ¼ tsp salt
- 2 minced cloves garlic
- 2 tsp lemon juice

Directions:

1. Preheat air fryer at 177°C/350°F.
2. Place salted water in a saucepan over high heat and bring it to a boil. Then, add in broccolini and boil for 3 minutes. Drain it and transfer it into a bowl.
3. Mix in butter, garlic, and salt.
4. Place the broccolini in the frying basket and Air Fry for 6 minutes.
5. Serve immediately garnished with lemon juice.

Variations & Ingredients Tips:

- Add grated parmesan or breadcrumbs for a crispy topping.
- Substitute olive oil for the butter to make it vegan/dairy-free.
- Toss with balsamic glaze or soy sauce before serving.

Per Serving: Calories: 140; Total Fat: 12g; Saturated Fat: 7g; Cholesterol: 30mg; Sodium: 380mg; Total Carbs: 7g; Fiber: 3g; Sugars: 2g; Protein: 3g

Veggie Fritters

Servings: 4 | Prep Time: 15 Minutes | Cooking Time: 35 Minutes

Ingredients:

- ¼ cup crumbled feta cheese
- 1 grated zucchini
- ¼ cup Parmesan cheese
- 2 tbsp minced onion
- 1 tbsp garlic powder
- 1 tbsp flour
- 1 tbsp cornmeal
- 1 tbsp butter, melted
- 1 egg
- 2 tsp chopped dill
- 2 tsp chopped parsley
- Salt and pepper to taste
- 1 cup bread crumbs

Directions:

1. Preheat air fryer at 175°C/350°F. Squeeze grated zucchini between paper towels to remove excess moisture. In a bowl, combine all ingredients except breadcrumbs. Form mixture into 12 balls, about 2 tbsp each. In a shallow bowl, add breadcrumbs. Roll each ball in breadcrumbs, covering all sides. Place fritters on an ungreased pizza pan. Place in the frying basket and air fry for 11 minutes, flipping once. Serve.

Variations & Ingredients Tips:

- Add grated carrots, sweet potatoes, or beets for a colorful twist.
- Use goat cheese, ricotta, or mozzarella instead of feta for a different flavor profile.
- Serve with tzatziki sauce, marinara sauce, or ranch dressing for dipping.

Per Serving: Calories: 264; Total Fat: 14g; Saturated Fat: 7g; Cholesterol: 74mg; Sodium: 566mg; Total Carbohydrates: 25g; Dietary Fiber: 2g; Total Sugars: 3g; Protein: 11g

Roasted Brussels Sprouts

Servings: 4 | Prep Time: 10 Minutes | Cooking Time: 25 Minutes

Ingredients:

- 1/2 cup balsamic vinegar
- 2 tablespoons honey
- 454g Brussels sprouts, halved lengthwise
- 2 slices bacon, chopped
- 1/2 teaspoon garlic powder
- 1 teaspoon salt
- 1 tablespoon extra-virgin olive oil
- 1/4 cup grated Parmesan cheese

Directions:

1. Preheat air fryer to 190°C/370°F.
2. In a saucepan, reduce the vinegar and honey over medium-low heat for 8-10 mins until a thick glaze forms.
3. In a bowl, toss Brussels sprouts, bacon, garlic powder, salt and oil.
4. Pour mixture into air fryer basket and cook for 10

mins, checking doneness. Cook 2-5 more mins until crispy and tender.
5. Transfer to a bowl and toss with balsamic glaze.
6. Top with grated Parmesan before serving.

Variations & Ingredients Tips:

- Use maple syrup instead of honey in the glaze.
- Add sliced shallots or red pepper flakes before roasting.
- Substitute pecans or walnuts for bacon.

Per Serving: Calories: 174; Total Fat: 8g; Saturated Fat: 2g; Cholesterol: 8mg; Sodium: 680mg; Total Carbohydrates: 21g; Dietary Fiber: 6g; Total Sugars: 11g; Protein: 7g

Lemony Green Bean Sauté

Servings: 6 | Prep Time: 10 Minutes | Cooking Time: 15 Minutes

Ingredients:

- 1 tbsp chopped cilantro
- 454g green beans, trimmed
- 1/2 red onion, sliced
- 2 tbsp olive oil
- Salt and pepper to taste
- 1 tbsp grapefruit juice
- 6 lemon wedges

Directions:

1. Preheat air fryer to 180°C/360°F.
2. Coat the green beans, red onion, olive oil, salt, pepper, cilantro and grapefruit juice in a bowl.
3. Pour the mixture into the air fryer and bake for 5 minutes.
4. Stir well and cook for 5 minutes more.
5. Serve with lemon wedges.

Variations & Ingredients Tips:

- Use orange or lime juice instead of grapefruit.
- Add sliced almonds or crumbled feta for crunch and flavor.
- Toss with balsamic vinegar before serving.

Per Serving: Calories: 65; Total Fat: 4g; Saturated Fat: 0.5g; Cholesterol: 0mg; Sodium: 30mg; Total Carbs: 7g; Dietary Fiber: 3g; Total Sugars: 3g; Protein: 2g

Honey-mustard Asparagus Puffs

Servings: 4 | Prep Time: 10 Minutes | Cooking Time: 35 Minutes

Ingredients:

- 8 asparagus spears
- 1/2 sheet puff pastry
- 2 tbsp honey mustard
- 1 egg, lightly beaten

Directions:

1. Preheat the air fryer to 190°C/375°F.
2. Spread the pastry with honey mustard and cut it into 8 strips.
3. Wrap the pastry, honey mustard-side in, around the asparagus.
4. Put a rack in the frying basket and lay the asparagus spears on the rack.
5. Brush all over pastries with beaten egg and air fry for 12-17 minutes or until the pastry is golden.
6. Serve.

Variations & Ingredients Tips:

- Use puff pastry sheets instead of sheets for easier wrapping.
- Brush with an egg wash before cooking for a shiny finish.
- Sprinkle with parmesan cheese before baking.

Per Serving: Calories: 148; Total Fat: 9g; Saturated Fat: 3g; Cholesterol: 77mg; Sodium: 321mg; Total Carbs: 14g; Dietary Fiber: 1g; Total Sugars: 5g; Protein: 4g

Zucchini Fries

Servings: 3 | Prep Time: 20 Minutes | Cooking Time: 12 Minutes

Ingredients:

- 1 large zucchini
- ½ cup all-purpose flour or tapioca flour
- 2 large eggs, well beaten
- 1 cup seasoned Italian-style dried bread crumbs (gluten-free, if a concern)
- Olive oil spray

Directions:

1. Preheat the air fryer to 200°C/400°F. Trim the zucchini

into a long rectangular block, taking off the ends and four "sides" to make this shape. Cut the block lengthwise into 3-cm-thick slices. Lay these slices flat and cut in half widthwise. Slice each of these pieces into 1.3-cm-thick batons. Set up and fill three shallow soup plates or small pie plates on your counter: one for the flour, one for the beaten eggs, and one for the bread crumbs. Set a zucchini baton in the flour and turn it several times to coat all sides. Gently shake off any excess flour, then dip it in the eggs, turning it to coat. Let any excess egg slip back into the rest, then set the baton in the bread crumbs and turn it several times, pressing gently to coat all sides, even the ends. Set aside on a cutting board and continue coating the remainder of the batons in the same way. Lightly coat the batons on all sides with olive oil spray. Set them in two flat layers in the basket, the top layer at a 90-degree angle to the bottom one, with a little air space between the batons in each layer. In the end, the whole thing will look like a crosshatch pattern. Air-fry undisturbed for 6 minutes. Use kitchen tongs to gently rearrange the batons so that any covered parts are now uncovered. The batons no longer need to be in a crosshatch pattern. Continue air-frying undisturbed for 6 minutes, or until lightly browned and crisp. Gently pour the contents of the basket onto a wire rack. Spread the batons out and cool for only a minute or two before serving.

Variations & Ingredients Tips:

- Use panko breadcrumbs or crushed potato chips for a crunchier coating.
- Add grated Parmesan cheese, garlic powder, or smoked paprika to the breadcrumb mixture for extra flavor.
- Serve with marinara sauce, ranch dressing, or garlic aioli for dipping.

Per Serving: Calories: 255; Total Fat: 6g; Saturated Fat: 1g; Cholesterol: 124mg; Sodium: 476mg; Total Carbohydrates: 38g; Dietary Fiber: 3g; Total Sugars: 4g; Protein: 11g

Sandwiches And Burgers Recipes

Chicken Apple Brie Melt

Servings: 3 | Prep Time: 10 Minutes | Cooking Time: 13 Minutes

Ingredients:

- 3 140 to 170-gram boneless skinless chicken breasts
- Vegetable oil spray
- 1½ teaspoons Dried herbes de Provence
- 85 grams Brie, rind removed, thinly sliced
- 6 Thin cored apple slices
- 3 French rolls (gluten-free, if a concern)
- 2 tablespoons Dijon mustard (gluten-free, if a concern)

Directions:

1. Preheat the air fryer to 190°C/375°F.
2. Lightly coat all sides of the chicken breasts with vegetable oil spray. Sprinkle the breasts evenly with the herbes de Provence.
3. When the machine is at temperature, set the breasts in the basket and air-fry undisturbed for 10 minutes.
4. Top the chicken breasts with the apple slices, then the cheese. Air-fry undisturbed for 2 minutes, or until the cheese is melty and bubbling.
5. Use a nonstick-safe spatula and kitchen tongs, for balance, to transfer the breasts to a cutting board. Set the rolls in the basket and air-fry for 1 minute to warm through. (Putting them in the machine without splitting them keeps the insides very soft while the outside gets a little crunchy.)
6. Transfer the rolls to the cutting board. Split them open lengthwise, then spread 1 teaspoon mustard on each cut side. Set a prepared chicken breast on the bottom

of a roll and close with its top, repeating as necessary to make additional sandwiches. Serve warm.

Variations & Ingredients Tips:

- Substitute the Brie with Camembert or another soft cheese of your choice.
- Use pears instead of apples for a different flavor profile.
- Add baby spinach or arugula for extra greens and nutrition.

Per Serving: Calories: 510; Cholesterol: 135mg; Total Fat: 19g; Saturated Fat: 8g; Sodium: 670mg; Total Carbohydrates: 41g; Dietary Fiber: 2g; Total Sugars: 6g; Protein: 45g

Reuben Sandwiches

Servings: 2 | Prep Time: 10 Minutes | Cooking Time: 11 Minutes

Ingredients:

- 225 grams Sliced deli corned beef
- 4 teaspoons Regular or low-fat mayonnaise (not fat-free)
- 4 Rye bread slices
- 2 tablespoons plus 2 teaspoons Russian dressing
- ½ cup Purchased sauerkraut, squeezed by the handful over the sink to get rid of excess moisture
- 55 grams (2 to 4 slices) Swiss cheese slices (optional)

Directions:

1. Set the corned beef in the basket, slip the basket into the machine, and heat the air fryer to 200°C/400°F. Air-fry undisturbed for 3 minutes from the time the basket is put in the machine, just to warm up the meat.
2. Use kitchen tongs to transfer the corned beef to a cutting board. Spread 1 teaspoon mayonnaise on one side of each slice of rye bread, rubbing the mayonnaise into the bread with a small flatware knife.
3. Place the bread slices mayonnaise side down on a cutting board. Spread the Russian dressing over the "dry" side of each slice. For one sandwich, top one slice of bread with the corned beef, sauerkraut, and cheese (if using). For two sandwiches, top two slices of bread each with half of the corned beef, sauerkraut, and cheese (if using). Close the sandwiches with the re-

maining bread, setting it mayonnaise side up on top.
4. Set the sandwich(es) in the basket and air-fry undisturbed for 8 minutes, or until browned and crunchy.
5. Use a nonstick-safe spatula, and perhaps a flatware fork for balance, to transfer the sandwich(es) to a cutting board. Cool for 2 or 3 minutes before slicing in half and serving.

Variations & Ingredients Tips:

- Substitute corned beef with pastrami for a classic New York deli taste.
- Use Thousand Island dressing instead of Russian dressing for a tangy, sweet flavor.
- Add sliced dill pickles or mustard to the sandwich for extra zing.

Per Serving (1 sandwich): Calories: 520; Cholesterol: 75mg; Total Fat: 30g; Saturated Fat: 9g; Sodium: 2020mg; Total Carbohydrates: 36g; Dietary Fiber: 4g; Total Sugars: 6g; Protein: 29g

Black Bean Veggie Burgers

Servings: 3 | Prep Time: 15 Minutes | Cooking Time: 10 Minutes

Ingredients:

- 1 cup Drained and rinsed canned black beans
- ⅓ cup Pecan pieces
- ⅓ cup Rolled oats (not quick-cooking or steel-cut; gluten-free, if a concern)
- 2 tablespoons (or 1 small egg) Pasteurized egg substitute, such as Egg Beaters (gluten-free, if a concern)
- 2 teaspoons Red ketchup-like chili sauce, such as Heinz
- ¼ teaspoon Ground cumin
- ¼ teaspoon Dried oregano
- ¼ teaspoon Table salt
- ¼ teaspoon Ground black pepper
- Olive oil
- Olive oil spray

Directions:

1. Preheat the air fryer to 200°C/400°F.
2. Put the beans, pecans, oats, egg substitute or egg, chili sauce, cumin, oregano, salt, and pepper in a food processor. Cover and process to a coarse paste that will hold its shape like sugar-cookie dough, adding olive oil in 1-teaspoon increments to get the mixture to blend

smoothly. The amount of olive oil is actually dependent on the internal moisture content of the beans and the oats. Figure on about 1 tablespoon (three 1-teaspoon additions) for the smaller batch, with proportional increases for the other batches. A little too much olive oil can't hurt, but a dry paste will fall apart as it cooks and a far-too-wet paste will stick to the basket.

3. Scrape down and remove the blade. Using clean, wet hands, form the paste into two 10 cm patties for the small batch, three 10 cm patties for the medium, or four 10 cm patties for the large batch, setting them one by one on a cutting board. Generously coat both sides of the patties with olive oil spray.
4. Set them in the basket in one layer. Air-fry undisturbed for 10 minutes, or until lightly browned and crisp at the edges.
5. Use a nonstick-safe spatula, and perhaps a flatware fork for balance, to transfer the burgers to a wire rack. Cool for 5 minutes before serving.

Variations & Ingredients Tips:

- Add finely chopped vegetables like bell peppers, onions, or carrots for extra flavor and nutrition.
- Experiment with different spices and herbs, such as smoked paprika, garlic powder, or cilantro.
- For a gluten-free version, ensure all ingredients are certified gluten-free.

Per Serving: Calories: 280; Cholesterol: 0mg; Total Fat: 15g; Saturated Fat: 2g; Sodium: 420mg; Total Carbohydrates: 28g; Dietary Fiber: 8g; Total Sugars: 2g; Protein: 10g

Asian Glazed Meatballs

Servings: 4 | Prep Time: 15 Minutes | Cooking Time: 10 Minutes

Ingredients:

- 1 large shallot, finely chopped
- 2 cloves garlic, minced
- 1 tablespoon grated fresh ginger
- 2 teaspoons fresh thyme, finely chopped
- 1½ cups brown mushrooms, very finely chopped (a food processor works well here)
- 2 tablespoons soy sauce
- freshly ground black pepper
- ½ kg ground beef
- ¼ kg ground pork
- 3 egg yolks
- 1 cup Thai sweet chili sauce (spring roll sauce)
- ¼ cup toasted sesame seeds
- 2 scallions, sliced

Directions:

1. Combine the shallot, garlic, ginger, thyme, mushrooms, soy sauce, freshly ground black pepper, ground beef and pork, and egg yolks in a bowl and mix the ingredients together. Gently shape the mixture into 24 balls, about the size of a golf ball.
2. Preheat the air fryer to 190°C/380°F.
3. Working in batches, air-fry the meatballs for 8 minutes, turning the meatballs over halfway through the cooking time. Drizzle some of the Thai sweet chili sauce on top of each meatball and return the basket to the air fryer, air-frying for another 2 minutes. Reserve the remaining Thai sweet chili sauce for serving.
4. As soon as the meatballs are done, sprinkle with toasted sesame seeds and transfer them to a serving platter. Scatter the scallions around and serve warm.

Variations & Ingredients Tips:

- Use a food processor to finely chop the mushrooms for better texture in the meatballs.
- Work in batches when air frying the meatballs to ensure even cooking and browning.
- Drizzle the Thai sweet chili sauce over the meatballs towards the end of cooking for a nice glaze.

Per Serving: Calories: 550; Cholesterol: 205mg; Total Fat: 32g; Saturated Fat: 11g; Sodium: 1300mg; Total Carbohydrates: 36g; Dietary Fiber: 2g; Total Sugars: 23g; Protein: 29g

Chicken Saltimbocca Sandwiches

Servings: 3 | Prep Time: 10 Minutes | Cooking Time: 11 Minutes

Ingredients:

- 3 140to 170-gram boneless skinless chicken breasts
- 6 Thin prosciutto slices
- 6 Provolone cheese slices
- 3 Long soft rolls, such as hero, hoagie, or Italian sub rolls (gluten-free, if a concern), split open lengthwise
- 3 tablespoons Pesto, purchased or homemade

(see the headnote)

Directions:

1. Preheat the air fryer to 200°C/400°F.
2. Wrap each chicken breast with 2 prosciutto slices, spiraling the prosciutto around the breast and overlapping the slices a bit to cover the breast. The prosciutto will stick to the chicken more readily than bacon does.
3. When the machine is at temperature, set the wrapped chicken breasts in the basket and air-fry undisturbed for 10 minutes, or until the prosciutto is frizzled and the chicken is cooked through.
4. Overlap 2 cheese slices on each breast. Air-fry undisturbed for 1 minute, or until melted. Take the basket out of the machine.
5. Smear the insides of the rolls with the pesto, then use kitchen tongs to put a wrapped and cheesy chicken breast in each roll.

Variations & Ingredients Tips:

- Use fresh mozzarella instead of provolone for a creamier texture.
- Add sliced tomatoes or roasted red peppers for extra flavor and nutrition.
- Substitute prosciutto with ham or bacon if desired.

Per Serving: Calories: 630; Cholesterol: 125mg; Total Fat: 32g; Saturated Fat: 11g; Sodium: 1580mg; Total Carbohydrates: 38g; Dietary Fiber: 2g; Total Sugars: 4g; Protein: 48g

White Bean Veggie Burgers

Servings: 3 | Prep Time: 15 Minutes | Cooking Time: 13 Minutes

Ingredients:

- 320 grams Drained and rinsed canned white beans
- 3 tablespoons Rolled oats (not quick-cooking or steel-cut; gluten-free, if a concern)
- 3 tablespoons Chopped walnuts
- 2 teaspoons Olive oil
- 2 teaspoons Lemon juice
- 1½ teaspoons Dijon mustard (gluten-free, if a concern)
- ¾ teaspoon Dried sage leaves
- ¼ teaspoon Table salt
- Olive oil spray
- 3 Whole-wheat buns or gluten-free whole-grain buns (if a concern), split open

Directions:

1. Preheat the air fryer to 200°C/400°F.
2. Place the beans, oats, walnuts, oil, lemon juice, mustard, sage, and salt in a food processor. Cover and process to make a coarse paste that will hold its shape, about like wet sugar-cookie dough, stopping the machine to scrape down the inside of the canister at least once.
3. Scrape down and remove the blade. With clean and wet hands, form the bean paste into two 10-cm patties for the small batch, three 10-cm patties for the medium, or four 10-cm patties for the large batch. Generously coat the patties on both sides with olive oil spray.
4. Set them in the basket with some space between them and air-fry undisturbed for 12 minutes, or until lightly brown and crisp at the edges. The tops of the burgers will feel firm to the touch.
5. Use a nonstick-safe spatula, and perhaps a flatware fork for balance, to transfer the burgers to a cutting board. Set the buns cut side down in the basket in one layer (working in batches as necessary) and air-fry undisturbed for 1 minute, to toast a bit and warm up. Serve the burgers warm in the buns.

Variations & Ingredients Tips:

- Use black beans, chickpeas, or lentils instead of white beans for a different flavor and color.
- Add grated carrots, zucchini, or beets to the burger mixture for extra nutrition and texture.
- Serve with your favorite burger toppings like lettuce, tomato, onion, and pickles.

Per Serving (1 burger): Calories: 350; Cholesterol: 0mg; Total Fat: 13g; Saturated Fat: 1g; Sodium: 520mg; Total Carbohydrates: 48g; Dietary Fiber: 9g; Total Sugars: 4g; Protein: 14g

Mexican Cheeseburgers

Servings: 4 | Prep Time: 20 Minutes | Cooking Time: 22 Minutes

Ingredients:

- 570 grams ground beef
- ¼ cup finely chopped onion
- ½ cup crushed yellow corn tortilla chips
- 1 (35-gram) packet taco seasoning
- ¼ cup canned diced green chilies

- 1 egg, lightly beaten
- 115 grams pepper jack cheese, grated
- 4 (30-cm) flour tortillas
- shredded lettuce, sour cream, guacamole, salsa (for topping)

Directions:

1. Combine the ground beef, minced onion, crushed tortilla chips, taco seasoning, green chilies, and egg in a large bowl. Mix thoroughly until combined – your hands are good tools for this. Divide the meat into four equal portions and shape each portion into an oval-shaped burger.
2. Preheat the air fryer to 190°C/370°F.
3. Air-fry the burgers for 18 minutes, turning them over halfway through the cooking time. Divide the cheese between the burgers, lower fryer to 170°C/340°F and air-fry for an additional 4 minutes to melt the cheese. (This will give you a burger that is medium-well. If you prefer your cheeseburger medium-rare, shorten the cooking time to about 15 minutes and then add the cheese and proceed with the recipe.)
4. While the burgers are cooking, warm the tortillas wrapped in aluminum foil in a 175°C/350°F oven, or in a skillet with a little oil over medium-high heat for a couple of minutes. Keep the tortillas warm until the burgers are ready.
5. To assemble the burgers, spread sour cream over three quarters of the tortillas and top each with some shredded lettuce and salsa. Place the Mexican cheeseburgers on the lettuce and top with guacamole. Fold the tortillas around the burger, starting with the bottom and then folding the sides in over the top. (A little sour cream can help hold the seam of the tortilla together.) Serve immediately.

Variations & Ingredients Tips:

- Use ground turkey or chicken for a leaner burger option.
- Substitute pepper jack cheese with Monterey Jack or cheddar cheese if preferred.
- Add sliced jalapeños or hot sauce to the burger mixture for extra heat.

Per Serving (1 burger): Calories: 780; Cholesterol: 165mg; Total Fat: 44g; Saturated Fat: 18g; Sodium: 1480mg; Total Carbohydrates: 51g; Dietary Fiber: 4g; Total Sugars: 4g; Protein: 46g

Perfect Burgers

Servings: 3 | Prep Time: 10 Minutes | Cooking Time: 13 Minutes

Ingredients:

- 510 grams 90% lean ground beef
- 1½ tablespoons Worcestershire sauce (gluten-free, if a concern)
- ½ teaspoon Ground black pepper
- 3 Hamburger buns (gluten-free if a concern), split open

Directions:

1. Preheat the air fryer to 190°C/375°F.
2. Gently mix the ground beef, Worcestershire sauce, and pepper in a bowl until well combined but preserving as much of the meat's fibers as possible. Divide this mixture into two 15-cm patties for the small batch, three 12.5-cm patties for the medium, or four 12.5-cm patties for the large. Make a thumbprint indentation in the center of each patty, about halfway through the meat.
3. Set the patties in the basket in one layer with some space between them. Air-fry undisturbed for 10 minutes, or until an instant-read meat thermometer inserted into the center of a burger registers 70°C/160°F (a medium-well burger). You may need to add 2 minutes cooking time if the air fryer is at 180°C/360°F.
4. Use a nonstick-safe spatula, and perhaps a flatware fork for balance, to transfer the burgers to a cutting board. Set the buns cut side down in the basket in one layer (working in batches as necessary) and air-fry undisturbed for 1 minute, to toast a bit and warm up. Serve the burgers in the warm buns.

Variations & Ingredients Tips:

- Mix in finely chopped onions, garlic, or herbs to the burger mixture for extra flavor.
- Use a mixture of ground beef and ground pork or lamb for a juicier, more flavorful burger.
- Top burgers with your favorite cheese, bacon, avocado, or sautéed mushrooms.

Per Serving (1 burger): Calories: 420; Cholesterol: 105mg; Total Fat: 22g; Saturated Fat: 8g; Sodium: 460mg; Total Carbohydrates: 23g; Dietary Fiber: 1g; Total Sugars: 3g; Protein: 34g

Chili Cheese Dogs

Servings: 3 | Prep Time: 10 Minutes | Cooking Time: 12 Minutes

Ingredients:

- 340 grams Lean ground beef
- 1½ tablespoons Chile powder
- 240 grams plus 2 tablespoons Jarred sofrito
- 3 Hot dogs (gluten-free, if a concern)
- 3 Hot dog buns (gluten-free, if a concern), split open lengthwise
- 3 tablespoons Finely chopped scallion
- 60 grams Shredded Cheddar cheese

Directions:

1. Crumble the ground beef into a medium or large saucepan set over medium heat. Brown well, stirring often to break up the clumps. Add the chile powder and cook for 30 seconds, stirring the whole time. Stir in the sofrito and bring to a simmer. Reduce the heat to low and simmer, stirring occasionally, for 5 minutes. Keep warm.
2. Preheat the air fryer to 200°C/400°F.
3. When the machine is at temperature, put the hot dogs in the basket and air-fry undisturbed for 10 minutes, or until the hot dogs are bubbling and blistered, even a little crisp.
4. Use kitchen tongs to put the hot dogs in the buns. Top each with about 120 grams of the ground beef mixture, 1 tablespoon of the minced scallion, and 20 grams of the cheese. (The scallion should go under the cheese so it superheats and wilts a bit.) Set the filled hot dog buns in the basket and air-fry undisturbed for 2 minutes, or until the cheese has melted.
5. Remove the basket from the machine. Cool the chili cheese dogs in the basket for 5 minutes before serving.

Variations & Ingredients Tips:

- Use turkey or veggie hot dogs for a healthier option.
- Substitute cheddar cheese with your favorite melty cheese, such as pepper jack or Swiss.
- Add diced onions or jalapeños to the chili for extra flavor and heat.

Per Serving: Calories: 580; Cholesterol: 110mg; Total Fat: 32g; Saturated Fat: 13g; Sodium: 1420mg; Total Carbohydrates: 36g; Dietary Fiber: 5g; Total Sugars: 6g; Protein: 38g

Salmon Burgers

Servings: 3 | Prep Time: 15 Minutes | Cooking Time: 8 Minutes

Ingredients:

- 510 grams Skinless salmon fillet, preferably fattier Atlantic salmon
- 1½ tablespoons Minced chives or the green part of a scallion
- ½ cup Plain panko bread crumbs (gluten-free, if a concern)
- 1½ teaspoons Dijon mustard (gluten-free, if a concern)
- 1½ teaspoons Drained and rinsed capers, minced
- 1½ teaspoons Lemon juice
- ¼ teaspoon Table salt
- ¼ teaspoon Ground black pepper
- Vegetable oil spray

Directions:

1. Preheat the air fryer to 190°C/375°F.
2. Cut the salmon into pieces that will fit in a food processor. Cover and pulse until coarsely chopped. Add the chives and pulse to combine, until the fish is ground but not a paste. Scrape down and remove the blade. Scrape the salmon mixture into a bowl. Add the bread crumbs, mustard, capers, lemon juice, salt, and pepper. Stir gently until well combined.
3. Use clean and dry hands to form the mixture into two 12.5-cm patties for a small batch, three 12.5-cm patties for a medium batch, or four 12.5-cm patties for a large one.
4. Coat both sides of each patty with vegetable oil spray. Set them in the basket in one layer and air-fry undisturbed for 8 minutes, or until browned and an instant-read meat thermometer inserted into the center of a burger registers 65°C/145°F.
5. Use a nonstick-safe spatula, and perhaps a flatware fork for balance, to transfer the burgers to a wire rack. Cool for 2 or 3 minutes before serving.

Variations & Ingredients Tips:

- Substitute salmon with canned or leftover cooked salmon for convenience.
- Add finely chopped red bell pepper or celery to the burger mixture for extra crunch and flavor.
- Serve on toasted buns with lettuce, tomato, and a dollop of tartar sauce or remoulade.

Per Serving (1 burger): Calories: 320; Cholesterol: 95mg; Total Fat: 16g; Saturated Fat: 3g; Sodium: 440mg; Total Carbohydrates: 15g; Dietary Fiber: 1g; Total Sugars: 1g; Protein: 31g

Best-ever Roast Beef Sandwiches

Servings: 6 | Prep Time: 10 Minutes | Cooking Time: 30-50 Minutes

Ingredients:

- 2½ teaspoons Olive oil
- 1½ teaspoons Dried oregano
- 1½ teaspoons Dried thyme
- 1½ teaspoons Onion powder
- 1½ teaspoons Table salt
- 1½ teaspoons Ground black pepper
- 1 kg Beef eye of round
- 6 Round soft rolls, such as Kaiser rolls or hamburger buns (gluten-free, if a concern), split open lengthwise
- ¾ cup Regular, low-fat, or fat-free mayonnaise (gluten-free, if a concern)
- 6 Romaine lettuce leaves, rinsed
- 6 Round tomato slices (0.5 cm thick)

Directions:

1. Preheat the air fryer to 180°C/350°F.
2. Mix the oil, oregano, thyme, onion powder, salt, and pepper in a small bowl. Spread this mixture all over the eye of round.
3. When the machine is at temperature, set the beef in the basket and air-fry for 30 to 50 minutes (the range depends on the size of the cut), turning the meat twice, until an instant-read meat thermometer inserted into the thickest piece of the meat registers 55°C/130°F for rare, 60°C/140°F for medium, or 65°C/150°F for well-done.
4. Use kitchen tongs to transfer the beef to a cutting board. Cool for 10 minutes. If serving now, carve into 3-mm-thick slices. Spread each roll with 2 tablespoons mayonnaise and divide the beef slices between the rolls. Top with a lettuce leaf and a tomato slice and serve. Or set the beef in a container, cover, and refrigerate for up to 3 days to make cold roast beef sandwiches anytime.

Variations & Ingredients Tips:

- Experiment with different herbs and spices in the rub, such as garlic powder, paprika, or rosemary.
- Add sliced red onions or pickles for extra flavor and crunch.
- Use leftover roast beef for cold sandwiches or salads.

Per Serving: Calories: 560; Cholesterol: 115mg; Total Fat: 27g; Saturated Fat: 6g; Sodium: 980mg; Total Carbohydrates: 32g; Dietary Fiber: 2g; Total Sugars: 4g; Protein: 47g

Inside Out Cheeseburgers

Servings: 2 | Prep Time: 15 Minutes | Cooking Time: 20 Minutes

Ingredients:

- 340 grams lean ground beef
- 3 tablespoons minced onion
- 4 teaspoons ketchup
- 2 teaspoons yellow mustard
- salt and freshly ground black pepper
- 4 slices of Cheddar cheese, broken into smaller pieces
- 8 hamburger dill pickle chips

Directions:

1. Combine the ground beef, minced onion, ketchup, mustard, salt and pepper in a large bowl. Mix well to thoroughly combine the ingredients. Divide the meat into four equal portions.
2. To make the stuffed burgers, flatten each portion of meat into a thin patty. Place 4 pickle chips and half of the cheese onto the center of two of the patties, leaving a rim around the edge of the patty exposed. Place the remaining two patties on top of the first and press the meat together firmly, sealing the edges tightly. With the burgers on a flat surface, press the sides of the burger with the palm of your hand to create a straight edge. This will help keep the stuffing inside the burger while it cooks.
3. Preheat the air fryer to 190°C/370°F.
4. Place the burgers inside the air fryer basket and air-fry for 20 minutes, flipping the burgers over halfway through the cooking time.
5. Serve the cheeseburgers on buns with lettuce and tomato.

Variations & Ingredients Tips:

- Use different types of cheese like Swiss, pepper jack, or blue cheese for a unique flavor.
- Add crispy bacon pieces or sautéed mushrooms to the stuffing for extra richness.
- Brush the burgers with a mixture of melted butter and minced garlic before cooking for added flavor.

Per Serving (1 burger): Calories: 510; Cholesterol: 145mg; Total Fat: 32g; Saturated Fat: 14g; Sodium: 780mg; Total Carbohydrates: 12g; Dietary Fiber: 1g; Total Sugars: 6g; Protein: 42g

Sausage And Pepper Heros

Servings: 3 | Prep Time: 10 Minutes | Cooking Time: 11 Minutes

Ingredients:

- 3 links (about 255 grams total) Sweet Italian sausages (gluten-free, if a concern)
- 1½ Medium red or green bell pepper(s), stemmed, cored, and cut into 1.25-cm-wide strips
- 1 medium Yellow or white onion(s), peeled, halved, and sliced into thin half-moons
- 3 Long soft rolls, such as hero, hoagie, or Italian sub rolls (gluten-free, if a concern), split open lengthwise
- For garnishing Balsamic vinegar
- For garnishing Fresh basil leaves

Directions:

1. Preheat the air fryer to 200°C/400°F.
2. When the machine is at temperature, set the sausage links in the basket in one layer and air-fry undisturbed for 5 minutes.
3. Add the pepper strips and onions. Continue air-frying, tossing and rearranging everything about once every minute, for 5 minutes, or until the sausages are browned and an instant-read meat thermometer inserted into one of the links registers 70°C/160°F.
4. Use a nonstick-safe spatula and kitchen tongs to transfer the sausages and vegetables to a cutting board. Set the rolls cut side down in the basket in one layer (working in batches as necessary) and air-fry undisturbed for 1 minute, to toast the rolls a bit and warm them up. Set 1 sausage with some pepper strips and onions in each warm roll, sprinkle balsamic vinegar over the sandwich fillings, and garnish with basil leaves.

Variations & Ingredients Tips:

- Use hot Italian sausage or chorizo for a spicier sandwich.
- Add sliced mushrooms or zucchini to the pepper and onion mixture for extra veggies.
- Top with shredded mozzarella or provolone cheese for a cheesy twist.

Per Serving (1 sandwich): Calories: 560; Cholesterol: 60mg; Total Fat: 36g; Saturated Fat: 12g; Sodium: 1420mg; Total Carbohydrates: 39g; Dietary Fiber: 3g; Total Sugars: 7g; Protein: 24g

Chicken Club Sandwiches

Servings: 3 | Prep Time: 15 Minutes | Cooking Time: 15 Minutes

Ingredients:

- 3 140- to 170-gram boneless skinless chicken breasts
- 6 Thick-cut bacon strips (gluten-free, if a concern)
- 3 Long soft rolls, such as hero, hoagie, or Italian sub rolls (gluten-free, if a concern)
- 3 tablespoons Regular, low-fat, or fat-free mayonnaise (gluten-free, if a concern)
- 3 Lettuce leaves, preferably romaine or iceberg
- 6 6-mm-thick tomato slices

Directions:

1. Preheat the air fryer to 190°C/375°F.
2. Wrap each chicken breast with 2 strips of bacon, spiraling the bacon around the meat, slightly overlapping the strips on each revolution. Start the second strip of bacon farther down the breast but on a line with the start of the first strip so they both end at a lined-up point on the chicken breast.
3. When the machine is at temperature, set the wrapped breasts bacon-seam side down in the basket with space between them. Air-fry undisturbed for 12 minutes, until the bacon is browned, crisp, and cooked through and an instant-read meat thermometer inserted into the center of a breast registers 75°C/165°F. You may need to add 2 minutes in the air fryer if the temperature is at 70°C/160°F.
4. Use kitchen tongs to transfer the breasts to a wire rack. Split the rolls open lengthwise and set them cut side down in the basket. Air-fry for 1 minute, or until

warmed through.

5. Use kitchen tongs to transfer the rolls to a cutting board. Spread 1 tablespoon mayonnaise on the cut side of one half of each roll. Top with a chicken breast, lettuce leaf, and tomato slice. Serve warm.

Variations & Ingredients Tips:

- Use turkey bacon for a lower-fat option.
- Add sliced avocado or pickled onions for extra flavor and texture.
- Toast the rolls before assembling the sandwiches for a crispy texture.

Per Serving: Calories: 640; Cholesterol: 110mg; Total Fat: 34g; Saturated Fat: 9g; Sodium: 1180mg; Total Carbohydrates: 44g; Dietary Fiber: 2g; Total Sugars: 5g; Protein: 42g

Eggplant Parmesan Subs

Servings: 2 | Prep Time: 10 Minutes | Cooking Time: 13 Minutes

Ingredients:

- 4 Peeled eggplant slices (about 1.25 cm thick and 7.5 cm in diameter)
- Olive oil spray
- 2 tablespoons plus 2 teaspoons Jarred pizza sauce, any variety except creamy
- ¼ cup (about 20 grams) Finely grated Parmesan cheese
- 2 Small, long soft rolls, such as hero, hoagie, or Italian sub rolls (gluten-free, if a concern), split open lengthwise

Directions:

1. Preheat the air fryer to 175°C/350°F.
2. When the machine is at temperature, coat both sides of the eggplant slices with olive oil spray. Set them in the basket in one layer and air-fry undisturbed for 10 minutes, until lightly browned and softened.
3. Increase the machine's temperature to 190°C/375°F (or 185°C/370°F, if that's the closest setting—unless the machine is already at 180°C/360°F, in which case leave it alone). Top each eggplant slice with 2 teaspoons pizza sauce, then 1 tablespoon of cheese. Air-fry undisturbed for 2 minutes, or until the cheese has melted.
4. Use a nonstick-safe spatula, and perhaps a flatware fork for balance, to transfer the eggplant slices cheese side up to a cutting board. Set the roll(s) cut side down in the basket in one layer (working in batches as necessary) and air-fry undisturbed for 1 minute, to toast the rolls a bit and warm them up. Set 2 eggplant slices in each warm roll.

Variations & Ingredients Tips:

- Use zucchini slices instead of eggplant for a different vegetable option.
- Add a slice of fresh mozzarella on top of the Parmesan for extra cheesiness.
- Sprinkle some dried herbs like oregano or basil on the eggplant before cooking for extra flavor.

Per Serving (1 sandwich): Calories: 280; Cholesterol: 10mg; Total Fat: 9g; Saturated Fat: 3g; Sodium: 840mg; Total Carbohydrates: 40g; Dietary Fiber: 5g; Total Sugars: 8g; Protein: 11g

Thanksgiving Turkey Sandwiches

Servings: 3 | Prep Time: 15 Minutes | Cooking Time: 10 Minutes

Ingredients:

- 1½ cups Herb-seasoned stuffing mix (not cornbread-style; gluten-free, if a concern)
- 1 Large egg white(s)
- 2 tablespoons Water
- 3 140- to 170-gram turkey breast cutlets
- Vegetable oil spray
- 4½ tablespoons Purchased cranberry sauce, preferably whole berry
- ⅛ teaspoon Ground cinnamon
- ⅛ teaspoon Ground dried ginger
- 4½ tablespoons Regular, low-fat, or fat-free mayonnaise (gluten-free, if a concern)
- 6 tablespoons Shredded Brussels sprouts
- 3 Kaiser rolls (gluten-free, if a concern), split open

Directions:

1. Preheat the air fryer to 190°C/375°F.
2. Put the stuffing mix in a heavy zip-closed bag, seal it, lay it flat on your counter, and roll a rolling pin over the bag to crush the stuffing mix to the consistency of rough sand. (Or you can pulse the stuffing mix to the desired consistency in a food processor.)
3. Set up and fill two shallow soup plates or small pie plates on your counter: one for the egg white(s),

whisked with the water until foamy; and one for the ground stuffing mix.

4. Dip a cutlet in the egg white mixture, coating both sides and letting any excess egg white slip back into the rest. Set the cutlet in the ground stuffing mix and coat it evenly on both sides, pressing gently to coat well on both sides. Lightly coat the cutlet on both sides with vegetable oil spray, set it aside, and continue dipping and coating the remaining cutlets in the same way.
5. Set the cutlets in the basket and air-fry undisturbed for 10 minutes, or until crisp and brown. Use kitchen tongs to transfer the cutlets to a wire rack to cool for a few minutes.
6. Meanwhile, stir the cranberry sauce with the cinnamon and ginger in a small bowl. Mix the shredded Brussels sprouts and mayonnaise in a second bowl until the vegetable is evenly coated.
7. Build the sandwiches by spreading about 1½ tablespoons of the cranberry mixture on the cut side of the bottom half of each roll. Set a cutlet on top, then spread about 3 tablespoons of the Brussels sprouts mixture evenly over the cutlet. Set the other half of the roll on top and serve warm.

Variations & Ingredients Tips:

- Use leftover roasted turkey instead of turkey cutlets for a post-Thanksgiving sandwich.
- Substitute Brussels sprouts with shredded cabbage or kale for a different texture and flavor.
- Add a slice of brie or provolone cheese to the sandwich for extra creaminess.

Per Serving: Calories: 530; Cholesterol: 75mg; Total Fat: 22g; Saturated Fat: 4g; Sodium: 1180mg; Total Carbohydrates: 53g; Dietary Fiber: 4g; Total Sugars: 15g; Protein: 33g

Philly Cheesesteak Sandwiches

Servings: 3 | Prep Time: 10 Minutes | Cooking Time: 9 Minutes

Ingredients:

- 340 grams Shaved beef
- 1 tablespoon Worcestershire sauce (gluten-free, if a concern)
- ¼ teaspoon Garlic powder
- ¼ teaspoon Mild paprika
- 6 tablespoons (45 grams) Frozen bell pepper strips (do not thaw)
- 2 slices, broken into rings Very thin yellow or white medium onion slice(s)
- 170 grams (6 to 8 slices) Provolone cheese slices
- 3 Long soft rolls such as hero, hoagie, or Italian sub rolls, or hot dog buns (gluten-free, if a concern), split open lengthwise

Directions:

1. Preheat the air fryer to 200°C/400°F.
2. When the machine is at temperature, spread the shaved beef in the basket, leaving a 1.25-cm perimeter around the meat for good air flow. Sprinkle the meat with the Worcestershire sauce, paprika, and garlic powder. Spread the peppers and onions on top of the meat.
3. Air-fry undisturbed for 6 minutes, or until cooked through. Set the cheese on top of the meat. Continue air-frying undisturbed for 3 minutes, or until the cheese has melted.
4. Use kitchen tongs to divide the meat and cheese layers in the basket between the rolls or buns. Serve hot.

Variations & Ingredients Tips:

- Use thinly sliced ribeye or sirloin steak instead of shaved beef for a more traditional texture.
- Add sliced mushrooms to the pepper and onion mixture for extra flavor and nutrition.
- Substitute provolone with American cheese or Cheez Whiz for a classic Philly taste.

Per Serving: Calories: 620; Cholesterol: 135mg; Total Fat: 32g; Saturated Fat: 15g; Sodium: 1320mg; Total Carbohydrates: 38g; Dietary Fiber: 2g; Total Sugars: 5g; Protein: 48g

Inside-out Cheeseburgers

Servings: 3 | Prep Time: 15 Minutes | Cooking Time: 9-11 Minutes

Ingredients:

- 510 grams 90% lean ground beef
- ¾ teaspoon Dried oregano
- ¾ teaspoon Table salt
- ¾ teaspoon Ground black pepper
- ¼ teaspoon Garlic powder
- 6 tablespoons (about 45 grams) Shredded Cheddar, Swiss, or other semi-firm cheese, or a purchased blend of shredded cheeses

- 3 Hamburger buns (gluten-free, if a concern), split open

Directions:

1. Preheat the air fryer to 190°C/375°F.
2. Gently mix the ground beef, oregano, salt, pepper, and garlic powder in a bowl until well combined without turning the mixture to mush. Form it into two 15-cm patties for the small batch, three for the medium, or four for the large.
3. Place 2 tablespoons of the shredded cheese in the center of each patty. With clean hands, fold the sides of the patty up to cover the cheese, then pick it up and roll it gently into a ball to seal the cheese inside. Gently press it back into a 12.5-cm burger without letting any cheese squish out. Continue filling and preparing more burgers, as needed.
4. Place the burgers in the basket in one layer and air-fry undisturbed for 8 minutes for medium or 10 minutes for well-done. (An instant-read meat thermometer won't work for these burgers because it will hit the mostly melted cheese inside and offer a hotter temperature than the surrounding meat.)
5. Use a nonstick-safe spatula, and perhaps a flatware fork for balance, to transfer the burgers to a cutting board. Set the buns cut side down in the basket in one layer (working in batches as necessary) and air-fry undisturbed for 1 minute, to toast a bit and warm up. Cool the burgers a few minutes more, then serve them warm in the buns.

Variations & Ingredients Tips:

▶ Mix different types of cheese like cheddar, mozzarella, and blue cheese for a flavorful combination.
▶ Add finely chopped bacon or caramelized onions to the cheese stuffing for extra richness.
▶ Serve with your favorite burger toppings like lettuce, tomato, onion, and pickles.

Per Serving (1 burger): Calories: 480; Cholesterol: 125mg; Total Fat: 27g; Saturated Fat: 11g; Sodium: 720mg; Total Carbohydrates: 22g; Dietary Fiber: 1g; Total Sugars: 3g; Protein: 38g

Dijon Thyme Burgers

Servings: 3 | Prep Time: 15 Minutes | Cooking Time: 18 Minutes

Ingredients:

- 450 grams lean ground beef
- ⅓ cup panko breadcrumbs
- ¼ cup finely chopped onion
- 3 tablespoons Dijon mustard
- 1 tablespoon chopped fresh thyme
- 4 teaspoons Worcestershire sauce
- 1 teaspoon salt
- freshly ground black pepper
- Topping (optional):
- 2 tablespoons Dijon mustard
- 1 tablespoon dark brown sugar
- 1 teaspoon Worcestershire sauce
- 115 grams sliced Swiss cheese, optional

Directions:

1. Combine all the burger ingredients together in a large bowl and mix well. Divide the meat into 4 equal portions and then form the burgers, being careful not to over-handle the meat. One good way to do this is to throw the meat back and forth from one hand to another, packing the meat each time you catch it. Flatten the balls into patties, making an indentation in the center of each patty with your thumb (this will help it stay flat as it cooks) and flattening the sides of the burgers so that they will fit nicely into the air fryer basket.
2. Preheat the air fryer to 190°C/370°F.
3. If you don't have room for all four burgers, air-fry two or three burgers at a time for 8 minutes. Flip the burgers over and air-fry for another 6 minutes.
4. While the burgers are cooking combine the Dijon mustard, dark brown sugar, and Worcestershire sauce in a small bowl and mix well. This optional topping to the burgers really adds a boost of flavor at the end. Spread the Dijon topping evenly on each burger. If you cooked the burgers in batches, return the first batch to the cooker at this time – it's ok to place the fourth burger on top of the others in the center of the basket. Air-fry the burgers for another 3 minutes.
5. Finally, if desired, top each burger with a slice of Swiss cheese. Lower the air fryer temperature to 165°C/330°F and air-fry for another minute to melt the cheese. Serve the burgers on toasted brioche buns, dressed the way you like them.

Variations & Ingredients Tips:

▶ Use ground turkey or chicken for a leaner burger option.
▶ Add minced garlic or finely chopped herbs like parsley or chives for extra flavor.
▶ Substitute panko breadcrumbs with regular breadcrumbs or oats for a different texture.

Per Serving (1 burger with cheese): Calories: 500; Cholesterol: 120mg; Total Fat: 27g; Saturated Fat: 11g; Sodium: 1180mg; Total Carbohydrates: 21g; Dietary Fiber: 1g; Total Sugars: 5g; Protein: 41g

Lamb Burgers

Servings: 3 | Prep Time: 15 Minutes | Cooking Time: 17 Minutes

Ingredients:

- 510 grams Ground lamb
- 3 tablespoons Crumbled feta
- 1 teaspoon Minced garlic
- 1 teaspoon Tomato paste
- ¾ teaspoon Ground coriander
- ¾ teaspoon Ground dried ginger
- Up to ⅛ teaspoon Cayenne
- Up to a ⅛ teaspoon Table salt (optional)
- 3 Kaiser rolls or hamburger buns (gluten-free, if a concern), split open

Directions:

1. Preheat the air fryer to 190°C/375°F.
2. Gently mix the ground lamb, feta, garlic, tomato paste, coriander, ginger, cayenne, and salt (if using) in a bowl until well combined, trying to keep the bits of cheese intact. Form this mixture into two 15-cm patties for the small batch, three 12.5-cm patties for the medium, or four 12.5-cm patties for the large.
3. Set the patties in the basket in one layer and air-fry undisturbed for 16 minutes, or until an instant-read meat thermometer inserted into one burger registers 70°C/160°F. (The cheese is not an issue with the temperature probe in this recipe as it was for the Inside-Out Cheeseburgers, because the feta is so well mixed into the ground meat.)
4. Use a nonstick-safe spatula, and perhaps a flatware fork for balance, to transfer the burgers to a cutting board. Set the buns cut side down in the basket in one layer (working in batches as necessary) and air-fry undisturbed for 1 minute, to toast a bit and warm up. Serve the burgers warm in the buns.

Variations & Ingredients Tips:

- Substitute feta with goat cheese or crumbled blue cheese for a different flavor profile.
- Add finely chopped mint or parsley to the lamb mixture for a fresh, herbal taste.
- Serve with tzatziki sauce, sliced cucumbers, and red onions for a Greek-inspired burger.

Per Serving (1 burger): Calories: 560; Cholesterol: 140mg; Total Fat: 34g; Saturated Fat: 15g; Sodium: 580mg; Total Carbohydrates: 25g; Dietary Fiber: 1g; Total Sugars: 3g; Protein: 38g

Thai-style Pork Sliders

Servings: 4 | Prep Time: 15 Minutes | Cooking Time: 15 Minutes

Ingredients:

- 310 grams Ground pork
- 2½ tablespoons Very thinly sliced scallions, white and green parts
- 4 teaspoons Minced peeled fresh ginger
- 2½ teaspoons Fish sauce (gluten-free, if a concern)
- 2 teaspoons Thai curry paste (see the headnote; gluten-free, if a concern)
- 2 teaspoons Light brown sugar
- ¾ teaspoon Ground black pepper
- 4 Slider buns (gluten-free, if a concern)

Directions:

1. Preheat the air fryer to 190°C/375°F.
2. Gently mix the pork, scallions, ginger, fish sauce, curry paste, brown sugar, and black pepper in a bowl until well combined. With clean, wet hands, form about 80 grams of the pork mixture into a slider about 6.5-cm in diameter. Repeat until you use up all the meat—3 sliders for the small batch, 4 for the medium, and 6 for the large. (Keep wetting your hands to help the patties adhere.)
3. When the machine is at temperature, set the sliders in the basket in one layer. Air-fry undisturbed for 14 minutes, or until the sliders are golden brown and caramelized at their edges and an instant-read meat thermometer inserted into the center of a slider registers 70°C/160°F.
4. Use a nonstick-safe spatula, and perhaps a flatware fork for balance, to transfer the sliders to a cutting board. Set the buns cut side down in the basket in one layer (working in batches as necessary) and air-fry undisturbed for 1 minute, to toast a bit and warm up. Serve the sliders warm in the buns.

Variations & Ingredients Tips:

- Use ground chicken or turkey for a leaner slider op-

- Substitute Thai curry paste with red curry paste or green curry paste for a different flavor profile.
- Serve with pickled vegetables, cilantro, and sriracha mayonnaise for extra Thai-inspired toppings.

Per Serving (1 slider): Calories: 240; Cholesterol: 65mg; Total Fat: 13g; Saturated Fat: 4g; Sodium: 490mg; Total Carbohydrates: 18g; Dietary Fiber: 1g; Total Sugars: 4g; Protein: 15g

Desserts And Sweets

Mixed Berry Pie

Servings: 4 | Prep Time: 15 Minutes | Cooking Time: 25 Minutes

Ingredients:

- 2/3 cup blackberries, cut into thirds
- 1/4 cup sugar
- 2 tbsp cornstarch
- 1/4 tsp vanilla extract
- 1/4 tsp peppermint extract
- 1/2 tsp lemon zest
- 1 cup sliced strawberries
- 1 cup raspberries
- 1 refrigerated piecrust
- 1 large egg

Directions:

1. Mix sugar, cornstarch, vanilla, peppermint and zest in a bowl.
2. Gently toss in all berries until coated. Pour into a greased baking dish.
3. On a surface, roll out dough into a 18-cm round. Cover dish with dough and crimp edges.
4. Cut 4 slits in the top to vent. Brush with beaten egg.
5. Preheat air fryer to 175°C/350°F.
6. Air fry for 15 mins until crust is golden and berries are bubbling.
7. Let cool 15 mins before serving warm.

Variations & Ingredients Tips:

- Use a graham cracker or cookie crust instead of pie dough.
- Add a crumble or streusel topping before baking.
- Serve with vanilla ice cream or whipped cream.

Per Serving: Calories: 244; Total Fat: 7g; Saturated Fat: 2g; Sodium: 145mg; Total Carbohydrates: 43g; Dietary Fiber: 5g; Total Sugars: 24g; Protein: 4g

Cheese Blintzes

Servings: 6 | Prep Time: 20 Minutes | Cooking Time: 10 Minutes

Ingredients:

- 1½ 210-gram package(s) farmer cheese
- 3 tablespoons Regular or low-fat cream cheese (not fat-free)
- 3 tablespoons Granulated white sugar
- ¼ teaspoon Vanilla extract
- 6 Egg roll wrappers
- 3 tablespoons Butter, melted and cooled

Directions:

1. Preheat the air fryer to 190°C/375°F.
2. Use a flatware fork to mash the farmer cheese, cream cheese, sugar, and vanilla in a small bowl until smooth.
3. Set one egg roll wrapper on a clean, dry work surface. Place ¼ cup of the filling at the edge closest to you, leaving a 1-cm gap before the edge of the wrapper. Dip your clean finger in water and wet the edges of the wrapper. Fold the perpendicular sides over the filling, then roll the wrapper closed with the filling inside. Set it aside seam side down and continue filling the remainder of the wrappers.

4. Brush the wrappers on all sides with the melted butter. Be generous. Set them seam side down in the basket with as much space between them as possible. Air-fry undisturbed for 10 minutes, or until lightly browned.
5. Use a nonstick-safe spatula to transfer the blintzes to a wire rack. Cool for at least 5 minutes or up to 20 minutes before serving.

Variations & Ingredients Tips:

- Add grated lemon or orange zest to the filling for a citrusy note.
- Serve with fresh berries, fruit compote, or sour cream.
- Sprinkle with powdered sugar before serving for extra sweetness.

Per Serving: Calories: 330; Total Fat: 23g; Saturated Fat: 13g; Sodium: 470mg; Total Carbohydrates: 19g; Dietary Fiber: 0g; Total Sugars: 9g; Protein: 14g

Chocolate Rum Brownies

Servings: 6 | Prep Time: 10 Minutes | Cooking Time: 30 Minutes + Cooling Time

Ingredients:

- 1/2 cup butter, melted
- 1 cup white sugar
- 1 tsp dark rum
- 2 eggs
- 1/2 cup flour
- 1/3 cup cocoa powder
- 1/4 tsp baking powder
- Pinch of salt

Directions:

1. Preheat air fryer to 175°C/350°F.
2. Whisk melted butter, eggs and rum until fluffy.
3. In another bowl, combine flour, sugar, cocoa, salt and baking powder.
4. Gradually stir dry ingredients into wet ingredients until blended.
5. Spoon batter into a greased cake pan.
6. Bake for 20 mins until a toothpick comes out clean.
7. Let cool, then cut and serve.

Variations & Ingredients Tips:

- Omit rum for kid-friendly brownies.
- Add chocolate chips or nuts to the batter.
- Dust with powdered sugar before serving.

Per Serving: Calories: 342; Total Fat: 16g; Saturated Fat: 9g; Sodium: 109mg; Total Carbohydrates: 46g; Dietary Fiber: 2g; Total Sugars: 31g; Protein: 4g

Magic Giant Chocolate Cookies

Servings: 2 | Prep Time: 10 Minutes | Cooking Time: 30 Minutes

Ingredients:

- 2 tbsp white chocolate chips
- 1/2 cup flour
- 1/8 tsp baking soda
- 1/4 cup butter, melted
- 1/4 cup light brown sugar
- 2 tbsp granulated sugar
- 2 eggs
- 2 tbsp milk chocolate chips
- 1/4 cup chopped pecans
- 1/4 cup chopped hazelnuts
- 1/2 tsp vanilla extract
- Salt to taste

Directions:

1. Preheat air fryer at 175°C/350°F.
2. In a bowl, combine all ingredients until well mixed.
3. Press cookie mixture onto a greased pizza pan.
4. Place pizza pan in air fryer basket and bake for 10 minutes.
5. Let cool completely for 10 minutes.
6. Turn over onto a plate and serve.

Variations & Ingredients Tips:

- Use different nut varieties like walnuts or almonds.
- Add dried fruit like cranberries or raisins.
- Drizzle with melted chocolate or caramel before serving.

Per Serving (1 cookie): Calories: 659; Total Fat: 40g; Saturated Fat: 16g; Sodium: 260mg; Total Carbohydrates: 70g; Dietary Fiber: 4g; Total Sugars: 39g; Protein: 10g

Cherry Cheesecake Rolls

Servings: 6 | Prep Time: 15 Minutes | Cooking Time: 30 Minutes

Ingredients:

- 1 can crescent rolls

- 110-g cream cheese
- 1 tbsp cherry preserves
- 1/3 cup sliced fresh cherries

Directions:

1. Roll out dough into a large rectangle and cut into 12 rectangles.
2. Microwave cream cheese 15 secs to soften. Mix with cherry preserves.
3. Mound 2 tsp cherry-cheese mix on each dough piece, leaving edges clear.
4. Top each with 2 tsp fresh cherries.
5. Roll into cylinders.
6. Preheat air fryer to 175°C/350°F.
7. Place rolls in greased air fryer basket. Spray with oil.
8. Bake 8 minutes. Let cool 2-3 minutes before removing.

Variations & Ingredients Tips:

- Use other fruit preserves like strawberry or blueberry.
- Add chopped nuts or chocolate chips to the filling.
- Brush with melted butter instead of oil spray.

Per Serving: Calories: 193; Total Fat: 10g; Saturated Fat: 4g; Sodium: 245mg; Total Carbohydrates: 22g; Dietary Fiber: 1g; Total Sugars: 10g; Protein: 4g

Coconut Rice Cake

Servings: 8 | Prep Time: 10 Minutes | Cooking Time: 30 Minutes

Ingredients:

- 1 cup all-natural coconut water
- 1 cup unsweetened coconut milk
- 1 teaspoon almond extract
- ¼ teaspoon salt
- 4 tablespoons honey
- cooking spray
- ¾ cup raw jasmine rice
- 2 cups sliced or cubed fruit

Directions:

1. In a medium bowl, mix together the coconut water, coconut milk, almond extract, salt, and honey.
2. Spray air fryer baking pan with cooking spray and add the rice.
3. Pour liquid mixture over rice.
4. Cook at 180°C/360°F for 15 minutes. Stir and cook for 15 minutes longer or until rice grains are tender.
5. Allow cake to cool slightly. Run a dull knife around edge of cake, inside the pan. Turn the cake out onto a platter and garnish with fruit.

Variations & Ingredients Tips:

- Use brown rice, black rice, or wild rice for a nuttier flavor and chewier texture.
- Add shredded coconut to the batter for extra coconut goodness.
- Drizzle with coconut syrup or condensed milk before serving.

Per Serving: Calories: 200; Total Fat: 5g; Saturated Fat: 4g; Sodium: 100mg; Total Carbohydrates: 36g; Dietary Fiber: 1g; Total Sugars: 15g; Protein: 2g

Holiday Pear Crumble

Servings: 4 | Prep Time: 15 Minutes | Cooking Time: 40 Minutes

Ingredients:

- 2 tbsp coconut oil
- 1/4 cup flour
- 1/4 cup demerara sugar
- 1/8 tsp salt
- 2 cups finely chopped pears
- 1/2 tbsp lemon juice
- 3/4 tsp cinnamon

Directions:

1. In a bowl, mix together coconut oil, flour, sugar and salt until crumbly.
2. Preheat air fryer to 160°C/320°F.
3. Stir together pears, 3 tbsp water, lemon juice and cinnamon in a baking pan.
4. Sprinkle chilled topping evenly over the pear mixture.
5. Bake for 30 minutes until pears are softened and topping is crispy.
6. Serve warm.

Variations & Ingredients Tips:

- Use apples or a mix of fruits instead of just pears.
- Add oats, nuts or spices like nutmeg to the crumble topping.
- Drizzle with caramel sauce before serving.

Per Serving: Calories: 233; Total Fat: 9g; Saturated Fat: 5g; Sodium: 58mg; Total Carbohydrates: 38g; Dietary Fiber: 4g; Total Sugars: 23g; Protein: 2g

Peanut Butter-banana Roll-ups

Servings: 4 | Prep Time: 10 Minutes | Cooking Time: 20 Minutes

Ingredients:

- 2 ripe bananas, halved crosswise
- 4 spring roll wrappers
- 1/4 cup molasses
- 1/4 cup peanut butter
- 1 tsp ground cinnamon
- 1 tsp lemon zest

Directions:

1. Preheat air fryer to 190°C/375°F.
2. Place the roll wrappers on a flat surface with one corner facing up.
3. Spread 1 tbsp of molasses on each, then 1 tbsp of peanut butter, and finally top with lemon zest and 1 banana half. Sprinkle with cinnamon all over.
4. For the wontons, fold the bottom over the banana, then fold the sides, and roll-up.
5. Place them seam-side down and Roast for 10 minutes until golden brown and crispy.
6. Serve warm.

Variations & Ingredients Tips:

- Use other nut butters like almond or cashew butter.
- Drizzle with honey before serving.
- Roll in crushed graham crackers or granola after baking.

Per Serving: Calories: 315; Total Fat: 12g; Saturated Fat: 2g; Cholesterol: 0mg; Sodium: 150mg; Total Carbs: 51g; Dietary Fiber: 4g; Total Sugars: 28g; Protein: 6g

Cinnamon Pear Cheesecake

Servings: 6 | Prep Time: 20 Minutes | Cooking Time: 60 Minutes + Cooling Time

Ingredients:

- 450-g cream cheese, softened
- 1 cup crumbled graham crackers
- 4 peeled pears, sliced
- 1 tsp vanilla extract
- 1 tbsp brown sugar
- 1 tsp ground cinnamon
- 1 egg
- 1 cup condensed milk
- 2 tbsp white sugar
- 1 1/2 tsp butter, melted

Directions:

1. Preheat air fryer to 175°C/350°F.
2. Mix graham cracker crumbs, white sugar and melted butter. Press into greased pan.
3. Bake crust for 5 minutes. Let cool 30 minutes to harden.
4. Beat cream cheese, vanilla, brown sugar, cinnamon, condensed milk and egg.
5. Arrange pear slices over crust and top with cream cheese mixture.
6. Bake for 40 minutes until set.
7. Allow to cool completely before serving.

Variations & Ingredients Tips:

- Use gingersnaps or biscoff cookies for the crust.
- Top with streusel or granola before baking.
- Substitute apple slices or mixed berries for the pears.

Per Serving: Calories: 508; Total Fat: 26g; Saturated Fat: 14g; Sodium: 424mg; Total Carbohydrates: 58g; Dietary Fiber: 2g; Total Sugars: 40g; Protein: 11g

Brown Sugar Baked Apples

Servings: 4 | Prep Time: 10 Minutes | Cooking Time: 15 Minutes

Ingredients:

- 3 Small tart apples, preferably McIntosh
- 4 tablespoons (1/4 cup/1/2 stick) Butter
- 6 tablespoons Light brown sugar
- Ground cinnamon
- Table salt

Directions:

1. Preheat the air fryer to 200°C/400°F.
2. Stem the apples, then cut them in half through their "equators". Use a melon baller to core the apples, creating a cavity in the center of each half.
3. Set the apple halves cut side up in the air fryer basket with space between them.
4. Drop 2 teaspoons of butter into the cavity of each apple half.
5. Sprinkle each half with 1 tablespoon brown sugar and a pinch each of ground cinnamon and table salt.

6. Return the basket to the air fryer. Air fry for 15 minutes undisturbed, until apples are softened and brown sugar is caramelized.
7. Use a nonstick spatula to transfer apple halves cut side up to a wire rack.
8. Cool for at least 10 minutes before serving, or serve at room temperature.

Variations & Ingredients Tips:

- Use a mix of different baking apples like Honeycrisp or Gala.
- Add chopped nuts like pecans or walnuts to the cavity.
- Drizzle with caramel sauce before serving.

Per Serving: Calories: 210; Total Fat: 9g; Saturated Fat: 5g; Sodium: 92mg; Total Carbohydrates: 33g; Dietary Fiber: 3g; Total Sugars: 27g; Protein: 1g

Rustic Berry Layer Cake

Servings: 6 | Prep Time: 15 Minutes | Cooking Time: 45 Minutes

Ingredients:

- 2 eggs, beaten
- 1/2 cup milk
- 2 tbsp Greek yogurt
- 1/4 cup maple syrup
- 1 tbsp apple cider vinegar
- 1 tbsp vanilla extract
- 3/4 cup all-purpose flour
- 1 tsp baking powder
- 1/2 tsp baking soda
- 1/4 cup dark chocolate chips
- 1/3 cup raspberry jam

Directions:

1. Preheat air fryer to 175°C/350°F.
2. Combine the eggs, milk, Greek yogurt, maple syrup, apple cider vinegar, and vanilla extract in a bowl.
3. Toss in flour, baking powder, and baking soda until combined.
4. Pour the batter into a 15cm round cake pan, distributing well, and Bake for 20-25 minutes until a toothpick comes out clean. Let cool completely.
5. Turn the cake onto a plate, cut lengthwise to make 2 equal layers. Set aside.
6. Add chocolate chips to a heat-proof bowl and Bake for 3 minutes until fully melted.
7. In the meantime, spread raspberry jam on top of the bottom layer, distributing well, and top with the remaining layer.
8. Once the chocolate is ready, stir in 1 tbsp of milk. Pour over the layer cake and spread well.
9. Cut into 6 wedges and serve immediately.

Variations & Ingredients Tips:

- Use other berry jams like strawberry or blueberry.
- Substitute dark chocolate with white or milk chocolate.
- Top with fresh berries and whipped cream.

Per Serving: Calories: 270; Total Fat: 8g; Saturated Fat: 3g; Cholesterol: 60mg; Sodium: 200mg; Total Carbs: 44g; Dietary Fiber: 2g; Total Sugars: 20g; Protein: 6g

Peach Cobbler

Servings: 4 | Prep Time: 15 Minutes | Cooking Time: 12 Minutes

Ingredients:

- 450g frozen peaches, thawed, with juice (do not drain)
- 6 tablespoons sugar
- 1 tablespoon cornstarch
- 1 tablespoon water
- Crust:
- 1/2 cup flour
- 1/4 teaspoon salt
- 3 tablespoons butter
- 1 1/2 tablespoons cold water
- 1/4 teaspoon sugar

Directions:

1. Place peaches, including juice, and sugar in air fryer baking pan. Stir to mix well.
2. In a small cup, dissolve cornstarch in the water. Stir into peaches.
3. In a medium bowl, combine the flour and salt. Cut in butter using knives or a pastry blender. Stir in the cold water to make a stiff dough.
4. On a floured board or wax paper, pat dough into a square or circle slightly smaller than your air fryer baking pan. Cut diagonally into 4 pieces.
5. Place dough pieces on top of peaches, leaving a tiny bit of space between the edges. Sprinkle very lightly with sugar, no more than about 1/4 teaspoon.
6. Cook at 180°C/360°F for 12 minutes, until fruit bub-

bles and crust browns.

Variations & Ingredients Tips:

- Use fresh peaches when in season for even better flavor.
- Sprinkle cinnamon or nutmeg over the peaches before adding the crust.
- Serve warm with a scoop of vanilla ice cream or dollop of whipped cream.

Per Serving: Calories: 270; Total Fat: 9g; Saturated Fat: 6g; Cholesterol: 25mg; Sodium: 180mg; Total Carbs: 46g; Dietary Fiber: 2g; Total Sugars: 29g; Protein: 2g

Brownies With White Chocolate

Servings: 6 | Prep Time: 10 Minutes | Cooking Time: 30 Minutes

Ingredients:

- 1/4 cup white chocolate chips
- 1/4 cup muscovado sugar
- 1 egg
- 2 tbsp white sugar
- 2 tbsp canola oil
- 1 tsp vanilla
- 1/4 cup cocoa powder
- 1/3 cup flour

Directions:

1. Preheat air fryer to 170°C/340°F.
2. Beat the egg with muscovado sugar and white sugar in a bowl.
3. Mix in the canola oil and vanilla.
4. Stir in cocoa powder and flour until just combined.
5. Gently fold in white chocolate chips.
6. Spoon the batter into a lightly greased pan.
7. Bake for about 20 minutes until set when lightly touched.
8. Let cool completely before slicing.

Variations & Ingredients Tips:

- Use semi-sweet or dark chocolate chips instead of white chocolate.
- Add chopped nuts like walnuts or pecans to the batter.
- Dust with powdered sugar before serving.

Per Serving: Calories: 181; Total Fat: 8g; Saturated Fat: 3g; Sodium: 24mg; Total Carbohydrates: 25g; Dietary Fiber: 1g; Total Sugars: 15g; Protein: 3g

Grilled Pineapple Dessert

Servings: 4 | Prep Time: 5 Minutes | Cooking Time: 12 Minutes

Ingredients:

- oil for misting or cooking spray
- 4 1-cm-thick slices fresh pineapple, core removed
- 1 tablespoon honey
- ¼ teaspoon brandy
- 2 tablespoons slivered almonds, toasted
- vanilla frozen yogurt or coconut sorbet

Directions:

1. Spray both sides of pineapple slices with oil or cooking spray. Place on grill plate or directly into air fryer basket.
2. Cook at 200°C/390°F for 6 minutes. Turn slices over and cook for an additional 6 minutes.
3. Mix together the honey and brandy.
4. Remove cooked pineapple slices from air fryer, sprinkle with toasted almonds, and drizzle with honey mixture.
5. Serve with a scoop of frozen yogurt or sorbet on the side.

Variations & Ingredients Tips:

- Substitute brandy with rum, bourbon, or orange liqueur.
- Add a pinch of cinnamon or cardamom to the honey mixture for extra spice.
- Serve over pound cake, angel food cake, or vanilla sponge cake.

Per Serving: Calories: 120; Total Fat: 4g; Saturated Fat: 0g; Sodium: 0mg; Total Carbohydrates: 22g; Dietary Fiber: 2g; Total Sugars: 18g; Protein: 2g

Homemade Chips Ahoy

Servings: 4 | Prep Time: 10 Minutes | Cooking Time: 20 Minutes

Ingredients:

- 1 tbsp coconut oil, melted
- 1 tbsp honey
- 1 tbsp milk
- 1/2 tsp vanilla extract

- 1/4 cup oat flour
- 2 tbsp coconut sugar
- 1/4 tsp salt
- 1/4 tsp baking powder
- 2 tbsp chocolate chips

Directions:

1. Combine coconut oil, honey, milk and vanilla in a bowl.
2. Add oat flour, coconut sugar, salt and baking powder. Stir until combined.
3. Fold in chocolate chips.
4. Preheat air fryer to 175°C/350°F.
5. Pour batter into a greased baking pan, leaving some space between portions.
6. Bake for 7 minutes until golden brown. Do not overbake.
7. Transfer to a cooling rack and serve chilled.

Variations & Ingredients Tips:

- Use dairy-free milk and vegan chocolate chips for a vegan version.
- Add chopped nuts or dried fruit to the batter.
- Replace coconut sugar with brown sugar or maple syrup.

Per Serving (3 cookies): Calories: 148; Total Fat: 6g; Saturated Fat: 4g; Sodium: 116mg; Total Carbohydrates: 21g; Dietary Fiber: 2g; Total Sugars: 9g; Protein: 2g

Blueberry Cheesecake Tartlets

Servings: 9 | Prep Time: 20 Minutes | Cooking Time: 6 Minutes

Ingredients:

- 170-g cream cheese, softened
- 1/4 cup sugar
- 1 egg
- 1/2 teaspoon vanilla extract
- Zest of 2 lemons, divided
- 9 mini graham cracker tartlet shells
- 2 cups blueberries
- 1/2 teaspoon ground cinnamon
- Juice of 1/2 lemon
- 1/4 cup apricot preserves

Directions:

1. Preheat air fryer to 165°C/330°F.
2. Mix cream cheese, sugar, egg, vanilla and zest of 1 lemon until smooth.
3. Pour into tartlet shells.
4. Air fry 3 tartlets at a time for 6 mins, rotating halfway.
5. Toss blueberries with cinnamon, remaining zest and lemon juice.
6. Melt apricot preserves and toss with blueberry mixture.
7. Top cooled tartlets with blueberry mixture.
8. Refrigerate until ready to serve.

Variations & Ingredients Tips:

- Use raspberries or strawberries instead of blueberries.
- Add a sprinkle of graham cracker crumbs on top.
- Substitute lemon curd for preserves.

Per Serving: Calories: 165; Total Fat: 8g; Saturated Fat: 4g; Sodium: 105mg; Total Carbohydrates: 20g; Dietary Fiber: 1g; Total Sugars: 13g; Protein: 3g

Fried Cannoli Wontons

Servings: 10 | Prep Time: 20 Minutes | Cooking Time: 8 Minutes

Ingredients:

- 227 grams Neufchâtel cream cheese
- ¼ cup powdered sugar
- 1 teaspoon vanilla extract
- ¼ teaspoon salt
- ¼ cup mini chocolate chips
- 2 tablespoons chopped pecans (optional)
- 20 wonton wrappers
- ¼ cup filtered water

Directions:

1. Preheat the air fryer to 190°C/370°F.
2. In a large bowl, use a hand mixer to combine the cream cheese with the powdered sugar, vanilla, and salt. Fold in the chocolate chips and pecans. Set aside.
3. Lay the wonton wrappers out on a flat, smooth surface and place a bowl with the filtered water next to them.
4. Use a teaspoon to evenly divide the cream cheese mixture among the 20 wonton wrappers, placing the batter in the center of the wontons.
5. Wet the tip of your index finger, and gently moisten the outer edges of the wrapper. Then fold each wrapper until it creates a secure pocket.
6. Liberally spray the air fryer basket with olive oil mist.
7. Place the wontons into the basket, and cook for 5 to 8 minutes. When the outer edges begin to brown, remove

the wontons from the air fryer basket. Repeat cooking with remaining wontons.
8. Serve warm.

Variations & Ingredients Tips:

- Use ricotta cheese or mascarpone instead of cream cheese for a more authentic flavor.
- Add a pinch of cinnamon or orange zest to the filling.
- Dust with powdered sugar or drizzle with chocolate sauce before serving.

Per Serving: Calories: 140; Total Fat: 8g; Saturated Fat: 4g; Sodium: 200mg; Total Carbohydrates: 14g; Dietary Fiber: 0g; Total Sugars: 5g; Protein: 4g

Cinnamon Tortilla Crisps

Servings: 4 | Prep Time: 5 Minutes | Cooking Time: 8 Minutes

Ingredients:

- 1 tortilla
- 2 tsp muscovado sugar
- 1/2 tsp cinnamon

Directions:

1. Preheat air fryer to 175°C/350°F.
2. Slice tortilla into 8 triangles.
3. Spray tortilla triangles with oil on both sides.
4. Sprinkle with muscovado sugar and cinnamon.
5. Lightly spray tops with more oil.
6. Place in a single layer in air fryer basket.
7. Air Fry for 5-6 minutes until light brown.
8. Serve warm.

Variations & Ingredients Tips:

- Use a cinnamon-sugar mixture instead of separate ingredients.
- Add a pinch of cayenne for a kick of heat.
- Drizzle with honey or agave after cooking.

Per Serving: Calories: 66; Total Fat: 2g; Saturated Fat: 0g; Sodium: 88mg; Total Carbohydrates: 12g; Dietary Fiber: 1g; Total Sugars: 3g; Protein: 1g

Blueberry Crisp

Servings: 6 | Prep Time: 10 Minutes | Cooking Time: 13 Minutes

Ingredients:

- 3 cups Fresh or thawed frozen blueberries
- 1/3 cup Granulated white sugar
- 1 tablespoon Instant tapioca
- 1/3 cup All-purpose flour
- 1/3 cup Rolled oats (not quick-cooking or steel-cut)
- 1/3 cup Chopped walnuts or pecans
- 1/3 cup Packed light brown sugar
- 5 tablespoons plus 1 teaspoon (2/3 stick) Butter, melted and cooled
- 3/4 teaspoon Ground cinnamon
- 1/4 teaspoon Table salt

Directions:

1. Preheat the air fryer to 200°C/400°F.
2. Mix the blueberries, granulated sugar, and instant tapioca in a 15cm, 18cm or 20cm round cake pan.
3. Set the pan in the basket and air-fry for 5 minutes, until blueberries begin to bubble.
4. Meanwhile, mix flour, oats, nuts, brown sugar, butter, cinnamon, and salt in a bowl.
5. When blueberries bubble, crumble flour mixture evenly on top.
6. Continue air-frying for 8 minutes until topping is browned and filling is bubbling.
7. Transfer pan to a wire rack and cool at least 10 minutes before serving.

Variations & Ingredients Tips:

- Use other berries like raspberries or blackberries.
- Add lemon or orange zest to the crisp topping.
- Serve warm with a scoop of vanilla ice cream.

Per Serving: Calories: 322; Total Fat: 15g; Saturated Fat: 6g; Sodium: 122mg; Total Carbohydrates: 45g; Dietary Fiber: 3g; Total Sugars: 25g; Protein: 4g

Guilty Chocolate Cookies

Servings: 6 | Prep Time: 10 Minutes | Cooking Time: 25 Minutes

Ingredients:

- 3 eggs, beaten
- 1 tsp vanilla extract
- 1 tsp apple cider vinegar
- 1/3 cup butter, softened
- 1/3 cup sugar

- ¼ cup cacao powder
- ¼ tsp baking soda

Directions:

1. Preheat air fryer to 150°C/300°F.
2. Combine eggs, vanilla extract, and apple vinegar in a bowl until well combined. Refrigerate for 5 minutes.
3. Whisk in butter and sugar until smooth, finally toss in cacao powder and baking soda until smooth.
4. Make balls out of the mixture. Place the balls onto the parchment-lined air fryer basket.
5. Bake for 13 minutes until brown.
6. Using a fork, flatten each cookie. Let cool completely before serving.

Variations & Ingredients Tips:

- Add chocolate chips, chopped nuts, or dried fruit to the dough for extra texture.
- Use coconut sugar or maple syrup instead of regular sugar for a healthier option.
- Serve with a glass of cold milk or a scoop of vanilla ice cream.

Per Serving: Calories: 220; Total Fat: 14g; Saturated Fat: 8g; Sodium: 140mg; Total Carbohydrates: 20g; Dietary Fiber: 2g; Total Sugars: 15g; Protein: 5g

Wild Blueberry Sweet Empanadas

Servings: 12 | Prep Time: 30 Minutes (includes Chilling Jam) | Cooking Time: 8 Minutes

Ingredients:

- 2 cups frozen wild blueberries
- 5 tablespoons chia seeds
- 1/4 cup honey
- 1 tablespoon lemon or lime juice
- 1/4 cup water
- 1 1/2 cups all-purpose flour
- 1 cup whole-wheat flour
- 1/2 teaspoon salt
- 1 tablespoon sugar
- 1/2 cup cold unsalted butter
- 1 egg
- 1/2 cup plus 2 tablespoons milk, divided
- 1 cup powdered sugar
- 1 teaspoon vanilla extract

Directions:

1. To make the wild blueberry chia jam, place the blueberries, chia seeds, honey, lemon or lime juice, and water into a blender and pulse for 2 minutes. Pour the chia jam into a glass jar or bowl and cover. Store in the refrigerator at least 4 to 8 hours or until the jam is thickened.
2. In a food processor, place the all-purpose flour, whole-wheat flour, salt, sugar, and butter and process for 2 minutes, scraping down the sides of the food processor every 30 seconds. Add in the egg and blend for 30 seconds. Using the pulse button, add in 1/2 cup of the milk 1 tablespoon at a time or until the dough is moist enough to handle and be rolled into a ball. Let the dough rest at room temperature for 30 minutes.
3. On a floured surface, cut the dough in half; then form a ball and cut each ball into 6 equal pieces, totaling 12 equal pieces. Work with one piece at a time, and cover the remaining dough with a towel. Roll out the dough into a 15cm round, with 6mm thickness. Place 4 tablespoons of filling in the center of round, fold over to form a half-circle. Using a fork, crimp the edges together and pierce the top with a fork for air holes. Repeat with the remaining dough and filling.
4. Preheat the air fryer to 175°C/350°F.
5. Working in batches, place 3 to 4 empanadas in the air fryer basket and spray with cooking spray. Cook for 8 minutes. Repeat in batches, as needed. Allow the sweet empanadas to cool for 15 minutes.
6. Meanwhile, in a small bowl, whisk together the powdered sugar, the remaining 2 tablespoons of milk, and the vanilla extract. Then drizzle the glaze over the surface and serve.

Variations & Ingredients Tips:

- Use other berry varieties like raspberries or blackberries.
- Dust with cinnamon-sugar before baking.
- Serve with vanilla ice cream or whipped cream.

Per Serving (1 empanada): Calories: 265; Total Fat: 11g; Saturated Fat: 6g; Cholesterol: 35mg; Sodium: 115mg; Total Carbs: 39g; Dietary Fiber: 4g; Total Sugars: 16g; Protein: 5g

INDEX

A

Apple French Toast Sandwich	10
Asian Glazed Meatballs	75
Asian-style Orange Chicken	34
Asian-style Salmon Fillets	55
Asy Carnitas	44

B

Baba Ghanouj	20
Bacon & Chicken Flatbread	36
Bacon Puff Pastry Pinwheels	15
Baked Eggs With Bacon-tomato Sauce	14
Balsamic Caprese Hasselback	58
Balsamic Short Ribs	39
Barbecue Chicken Nachos	24
Basil Feta Crostini	23
Best-ever Roast Beef Sandwiches	79
Black Bean Veggie Burgers	75
Black Cod With Grapes, Fennel, Pecans And Kale	53
Blossom Bbq Pork Chops	46
Blueberry Cheesecake Tartlets	91
Blueberry Crisp	92
Breaded Mozzarella Sticks	18
Breaded Parmesan Perch	55
Brown Rice And Goat Cheese Croquettes	66
Brown Sugar Baked Apples	89
Brownies With White Chocolate	90
Buttered Garlic Broccolini	71

C

Cal-mex Chimichangas	42
Caprese-style Sandwiches	57
Charred Cauliflower Tacos	57
Cheddar & Sausage Tater Tots	12
Cheddar Stuffed Portobellos With Salsa	64

Cheese & Crab Stuffed Mushrooms	53	Citrusy Brussels Sprouts	68
Cheese Blintzes	86	Coconut Rice Cake	87
Cheesy Zucchini Chips	22	Corn & Shrimp Boil	55
Cherry Cheesecake Rolls	87	Corn On The Cob	68
Chicken Apple Brie Melt	74	Crab Cakes On A Budget	52
Chicken Club Sandwiches	81	Crab Toasts	25
Chicken Cordon Bleu Patties	28	Crabmeat-stuffed Flounder	48
Chicken Flautas	31	Crispy Chicken Bites With Gorgonzola Sauce	24
Chicken Fried Steak With Gravy	32	Crispy Chicken Cakes	18
Chicken Nachos	26	Crispy Duck With Cherry Sauce	27
Chicken Salad With White Dressing	31	Crispy Fish Sandwiches	49
Chicken Saltimbocca Sandwiches	76	Crustless Broccoli, Roasted Pepper And Fontina Quiche	13
Chicken Schnitzel Dogs	33		
Chicken-fried Steak	45		

D

Dijon Thyme Burgers	83

Chili Cheese Dogs	78		
Chocolate Rum Brownies	86		

E

Egg & Bacon Pockets	12
Eggplant Parmesan Subs	81

Chorizo Biscuits	16		
Cinnamon Apple Crisps	21		
Cinnamon Pear Cheesecake	88		

F

Fiery Chicken Meatballs	35
Fiery Sweet Chicken Wings	26

Cinnamon Pear Oat Muffins	15		
Cinnamon Tortilla Crisps	92		

Fiesta Chicken Plate	28
Flank Steak With Roasted Peppers And Chimichurri	43
Fried Cannoli Wontons	92
Fried Olives	19
Fried Rice With Curried Tofu	63
Fried Scallops	48

G

Garlicky Bell Pepper Mix	67
Garlicky Roasted Mushrooms	57
German-style Pork Patties	45
Glazed Carrots	66
Granola	11
Greek Pork Chops	37
Greek Street Tacos	21
Grilled Pineapple Dessert	90
Guajillo Chile Chicken Meatballs	33
Guilty Chocolate Cookies	93

H

Ham & Cheese Sandwiches	10
Hashbrown Potatoes Lyonnaise	13
Hasselbacks	69
Herb-crusted Sole	47
Holiday Breakfast Casserole	11
Holiday Pear Crumble	87
Homemade Chips Ahoy	91
Honey Mesquite Pork Chops	40
Honey-mustard Asparagus Puffs	72
Honey-roasted Parsnips	71
Huevos Rancheros	16

I

Inside Out Cheeseburgers	80
Inside-out Cheeseburgers	83

K

Kid's Flounder Fingers	53
Korean-style Lamb Shoulder Chops	38

L

Lamb Burgers	84
Lemon Herb Whole Cornish Hen	36
Lemony Green Bean Sauté	72
Lentil Fritters	60

M

Magic Giant Chocolate Cookies	86
Malaysian Shrimp With Sambal Mayo	50
Meat Loaves	45
Meaty Omelet	14
Mediterranean Roasted Vegetables	70
Mediterranean Sea Scallops	50
Mexican Cheeseburgers	77
Mexican Twice Air-fried Sweet Potatoes	56
Mixed Berry Pie	85
Mom's Chicken Wings	31
Morning Burrito	15
Morning Potato Cakes	16
Moroccan-style Chicken Strips	29
Mozzarella Sticks	22

N

Nashville Hot Chicken	32

O

Oyster Shrimp With Fried Rice	50

P

Pancake Muffins	10
Panko-breaded Cod Fillets	54
Peach Cobbler	90
Peanut Butter-banana Roll-ups	88
Perfect Burgers	77
Perfect Pork Chops	38
Pesto Pepperoni Pizza Bread	61
Philly Cheesesteak Sandwiches	82
Pickle Brined Fried Chicken	30
Pinto Bean Casserole	63
Poblano Bake	36
Pork Chops	41
Pork Chops With Cereal Crust	46
Pork Schnitzel	40
Pork Schnitzel With Dill Sauce	43
Powerful Jackfruit Fritters	62

R

Reuben Sandwiches	74
Rich Clam Spread	25
Rich Spinach Chips	65

Rigatoni With Roasted Onions, Fennel, Spinach And Lemon Pepper Ricotta 59

Roasted Brussels Sprouts 72

Roasted Ratatouille Vegetables 70

Roasted Vegetable Thai Green Curry 61

Roasted Vegetable, Brown Rice And Black Bean Burrito 62

Roasted Yellow Squash And Onions 68

Rustic Berry Layer Cake 89

S

Salmon Burgers 78

Santorini Steak Bowls 41

Sausage And Pepper Heros 80

Shoestring Butternut Squash Fries 70

Shrimp Sliders With Avocado 47

Shrimp, Chorizo And Fingerling Potatoes 51

Simple Zucchini Ribbons 65

Sirloin Steak Bites With Gravy 38

Sloppy Joes 39

Smashed Fried Baby Potatoes 69

Smoked Whitefish Spread 19

Spanish Fried Baby Squid 22

Spiced Pumpkin Wedges 67

Spiced Vegetable Galette 59

Spicy Black Bean Turkey Burgers With Cumin-avocado Spread 29

Spinach & Brie Frittata 59

Spinach Cups 20

Summer Sea Scallops 51

Sweet Chili Spiced Chicken 34

Sweet Potato Chips 25

Sweet Potato–wrapped Shrimp 54

Sweet Roasted Carrots 60

Sweet-and-salty Pretzels 21

Sweet-hot Pepperoni Pizza 17

T

Teriyaki Chicken Legs 35

Tex-mex Potatoes With Avocado Dressing 63

Thai Peanut Veggie Burgers 58

Thai-style Pork Sliders 84

Thanksgiving Turkey Sandwiches 82

The Best Oysters Rockefeller 52

Thyme Meatless Patties	64
Tuna Nuggets In Hoisin Sauce	48
Tuscan Toast	17
Tuscan Veal Chops	42

V

Vegetarian Fritters With Green Dip	23
Veggie Fritters	71
Venison Backstrap	41
Vietnamese Gingered Tofu	64
Viking Toast	13

W

White Bean Veggie Burgers	76
Wild Blueberry Sweet Empanadas	93
Wrapped Shrimp Bites	26

Z

Za'atar Chicken Drumsticks	27
Zucchini Fries	73

Printed in Great Britain
by Amazon